The London Cuckolds

Three beautiful wives, three ludricrous husbands and one overly ambitious rake are the seductive and infallibly comic ingredients of this splendidly irreverent farce.

First performed in 1681, *The London Cuckolds* was an instant success and regularly revived for several decades. Three centuries later, Terry Johnson's new adaptation proves this seminal comedy to be the *No Sex Please, We're British* of Restoration theatre.

Terry Johnson's plays include *Amabel* (Bush, London, 1979); *Days Here So Dark* (Paines Plough at the Tricycle, London, 1981); *Insignificance* (Royal Court, London, 1982 and filmed by Nicholas Roeg, 1985); *Cries from the Mammal House* (Open Heart Enterprises with the Royal Court, London, 1984; *Unsuitable for Adults* (Bush, London, 1984); *Tuesday's Child*, written with Kate Lock (Theatre Royal, Stratford East, 1985); *Imagine Drowning* (Hampstead Theatre, London, 1991 and three-part adaptation for BBC TV, 1991); *Hysteria* (Royal Court, London, 1993; Duke of York's Theatre as part of the Royal Court Classics season, 1995); *Dead Funny* (Hampstead Theatre, 1994).

THE LONDON CUCKOLDS

by Edward Ravenscroft, Gent.
in a version by Terry Johnson

Methuen Drama

Copyright © 1998 by Terry Johnson
The right of Terry Johnson to be identified as the author of this work
has been asserted by him in accordance with
the Copyright, Designs and Patents Act, 1988

First published in the Great Britain in 1998
by Methuen Drama

A CIP catalogue record for this book is available from the British Library

Papers used by Methuen Drama are natural, recyclable products
made from wood grown in sustainable forests. The manufacturing processes
conform to the environmental regulations of the country of origin.

ISBN 0 413 72950 8

Typeset by MATS, Southend-on-Sea, Essex

The London Cuckolds

The London Cuckolds was first performed in the Lyttelton Auditorium of the Royal National Theatre on 13 February 1998. The cast was as follows:

Wiseacres	Robin Soans
Peggy	Kelly Reilly
Doodle	Anthony O'Donnell
Arabella	Caroline Quentin
Dashwell	William Chubb
Eugenia	Sharon Small
Ramble	Ben Miles
Townley	Nigel Lindsay
Loveday	Alexander Hanson
Aunt	Hilda Braid
Engine	Charon Bourke
Jane	Ysobel Gonzalez
Roger	Joseph Murray
Tom	Malcolm Browning
Coachman/1st Chimney-Sweep	Roger Swaine
Scullery Boy/2nd Chimney-Sweep	Morgan Symes
1st Watchman	Richard Addison
2nd Watchman	Simon Markey
Lamp Boy/3rd Watchman	Tom Peters
1st Servant	Virginia Hatton
2nd Servant	Kate Dyson

Directed by Terry Johnson
Designed by William Dudley
Lighting by Simon Corder
Music by Roger Skeaping
Sound by Colin Pink
Staff Director Charlotte Conquest
Stage Manager David Milling
Deputy Stage Manager Emma Gordon
Assistant Stage Manager Katy de Main
Assistant Stage Manager Michele Enright
Assistant Stage Manager Richard Reddrop

Characters

Wiseacres, *an Alderman of London*
Peggy, *bride to Wiseacres, an Innocent, and Country-bred*
Doodle, *an Alderman of London*
Arabella, *wife to Doodle, a Pretender to Wit*
Dashwell, *a City Scrivener*
Eugenia, *wife to Dashwell, a hypocrite*
Ramble, *a great Designer on Ladies, but unsuccessful in his intrigues*
Townley, *a Gentleman of the times, careless of women, but fortunate*
Loveday, *a Young Merchant, formerly a lover of Eugenia*
Aunt, *Governess to Peggy*
Engine, *Woman to Arabella*
Jane, *Eugenia's Maid*
Roger, *Footman to Ramble*
Tom, *Footman to Townley*
Lamp boy
Vendor
Two Chimney-Sweeps
Three Watchmen
Scullery Boy
Servants

Prologue

Spoken by **Arabella**

Well, now's your time, my masters of the pit
You that delights in women, wine and wit.
All things this evening jump for your delight
In mirth we wear the day, in love the night.
The theatre is open, and 'twould be to our cost
To strive and fail to please you most.
You gallants and you nymphs shall laugh
To see those struggle who have chose the married path
And those who sit with boosy husbands or with pinch-lipped
wives
Might look downcast should we dare criticise
The Mansion house of marriage, that never gives content
Like the convenient modish tenement
Of love, that's held by moderate lease or yearly rent.
But ladies, if with me you would your counsel join,
We'll make our tenants pay a swinging fine.
For if you drain your keeper 'til he's poor
And have the wit to lay it up in store
He must marry you in hope to mend his life
For what he lost to a mistress he must gain by a wife!
As for the rest, be not severe with us, but laugh;
For 'twould be folly to condemn what one glimpses in a glass.

(As for you critics, we are glad to see you in such number
And hope that in the least we do not disturb your slumber
Also praying we have had the wit
To sit you just precisely where you each prefer to sit.)

Act One

Scene One

The street before **Doodle**'s *house.*

Enter **Alderman Wiseacres** *and* **Doodle**.

Wiseacres Well, Mr Alderman Doodle, you promise to go along with me?

Doodle Yes. I will dispense with business on this occasion. Who else goes?

Wiseacres Only our neighbour Mr Dashwell.

Doodle We'll be going as soon as the Exchange closes?

Wiseacres Yes, and you shall then see the most simple innocent thing of a wife.

Doodle What? Is she simple you say?

Wiseacres Indeed she is silly. A mere infant in her intellects. But for her bigness you'd think her a baby.

Doodle How old is she?

Wiseacres But fourteen.

Doodle An infant to you indeed; why, you are above fifty.

Wiseacres What of it?

Doodle But a discreet woman of thirty had been more suitable for you.

Wiseacres But my intention is to marry a woman that will be young when I am old. I am convinced that an old man can never love an old woman. Age is a sore decayer and renders men backward in their duty, therefore I am marrying a woman so young that she might be a temptation to me when I am old. Perfumes, oils and oysters are nothing comparable to youth and beauty.

Doodle   So that's your drift.

Wiseacres   I have long lived a bachelor. I begin late, so would lengthen out my satisfaction as far as I'm able.

Doodle   But why do you marry one so silly; where's the satisfaction in that?

Wiseacres   Because a young wife that has wit would play the Devil with an old husband. Even the young husbands have trouble keeping them true nowadays.

Doodle   In this City, certainly.

Wiseacres   Therefore I chose a girl of four years of age that had no signs of wit. Her father and mother were none of the wisest either and, fortunately, dead. I placed the child in the care of her aunt, a somewhat decayed gentlewoman who was also a bit soft. I placed them in the country, at a lone house, and instructed her to bring the girl up in all simplicity and never to let her play amongst Boys. Now she's been moulded to my instruction I shall reap the fruits of my labour.

Doodle   But were there not fools enough of Heaven's making?

Wiseacres   Yes, but such grow wiser by experience and by the time they come to twenty years of age are quite another thing. This forward age ripens them apace. Thus I have bred a fool and marry her so young she never shall grow wiser.

Doodle   But should a wife not be a companion to a man? Would you have your wife a slave?

Wiseacres   Much rather than be a slave to a wife. A witty wife is the greatest plague on earth; she will have so many tricks and inventions to deceive a husband, he might never sleep for keeping watch upon his honour. From all which cares and troubles he is freed that has married a wife without the wit to offend.

Doodle   But if my wife was a fool I should always suspect *her* a whore, for 'tis want of wit that makes 'em believe the flatteries of men. I tell you, Mr Alderman; a woman without sense is like a castle without soldiers, to be taken at every assault.

Wiseacres   But I say still; wit is a dangerous weapon in a woman.

Doodle   I tell you, Brother Wiseacres, you are in the wrong.

Wiseacres   I tell you, Brother Doodle, I am in the right. You have a witty wife; much good may it do you.

Doodle   And much good to you and your fool!

Wiseacres   Better a fool than a wanton!

Doodle   Better a wanton than both!

Enter **Dashwell**.

Wiseacres   Your insistence provokes me!

Doodle   And your want of reason provokes me!

Wiseacres   I hope you will allow a witty wife may be a slut!

Doodle   And a foolish wife will certainly be one!

Dashwell   What has raised this heat between you?

Wiseacres   Oh, Mr Dashwell, in good time. You shall be judge now. We are in dispute here as to whether 'tis best for a man to have a laughing little giggling, highty, tighty, prattling, tattling, gossiping wife; such a one as he has married . . . ?

Doodle   Or a simple, sneaking, bashful, awkward, ill-bred country girl who wouldn't say boo to a goose, who can only answer ay *forsooth* and no *forsooth*, and stands in awe of her chambermaid! Such a one as Alderman Wiseacres here has taken pains to rear for his own proper use.

Wiseacres   What need my wife have wit to make her loud, talkative and impertinent when I have enough for her and myself too?

Doodle   Mr Dashwell; which of us do you think is in the right?

Dashwell   In the right?

Doodle   Ay.

Dashwell   Why, I think you both in the wrong.

Wiseacres   Both in the wrong!

Doodle   How can that be?

Dashwell   A wife that has wit will outwit her husband, and she that has no wit will be outwitted by those who wish to outwit him. So as to which will make her husband a cuckold first or oftenest; 'tis an even bet, if you would lay one.

Wiseacres   You are a married man, Mr Dashwell; what course have you taken?

Doodle   Ay; is yours wise or foolish?

Dashwell   Security lies not in the wise or the foolish but in the Godly wife.

Wiseacres   Oh, the Godly wife.

Dashwell   One that prays and goes often to church. Such a one have I.

Doodle   Sheer hypocrites all. How many cuckolds must there be in a parish whose bell tolls out their wives twice a day for assignations!

Wiseacres   Nor should my wife be taught catechism by some smooth-faced priest; Heaven knows what doctrine he may put into her!

Doodle   Much good may your Godly wife do you!

Dashwell   The world has never been of one mind since there was more than one man in it, and never will be so long as there are two. But to our business; I must go and acquaint my wife I'm going out of town, so shall meet you at Garraways coffee-house.

Doodle   The coffee-house.

Dashwell *exits.*

Wiseacres   Mr Alderman, you need not acquaint your wife with news of my marriage, for *my* wife shall be no gossiper nor woman of the times. I shall marry her tomorrow morning in private and in private she shall live.

Doodle   As you please.

Wiseacres   The coffee-house, then.

Doodle   The coffee-house.

Exit **Wiseacres**.

I dare not think what sport my wife would make of him should she have heard this odd humour.

He opens a door and **Arabella** *and* **Engine**, *who have been listening, tumble in.*

Arabella/Engine   Ha ha ha ha ha ha.

Doodle   Thou art very merry, wife.

Arabella   Ha ha ha.

Doodle   Prithee what dost thou laugh at?

Arabella   Lord, husband. If *your* wife was but a fool I am certain there would be no sense in the house!

Doodle   You overheard our discourse?

Arabella   He had a fling at me too, but I'll be revenged if ever I can come to speak to his silly wife. I'll read her a chapter of wisdom shall clear her understanding. How far off is this pattern of innocence?

Doodle   But a few hours from London.

Arabella   And you are to go upon this piece of gallantry to fetch the lady?

Doodle   He desired and I have promised.

Arabella   Are we to expect you home at dinner?

Doodle   No, we shall dine together in the city, then take the coach. Well, wife, you shan't see me again 'til tomorrow. There's a kiss to remember me. Adieu.

Arabella   Adieu, husband.

Exit **Doodle**.

Arabella   A kiss! Slender diet to live upon until tomorrow. I have a mind to feast in his absence upon lustier fare than a dull city husband. Engine, durst I pursue my inclinations with the man you have often heard me speak of?

Engine   A little variety, madam, would be pleasant. Always to feed upon an Alderman's flesh must be enough to cloy your stomach.

Arabella   He's so sparing with it, I'm never less than starving.

Engine   The better you're allowed to look abroad. Troth, madam, you must never lose your longing.

Arabella   Thou shalt go to him. Thou hast a pretty good way of speaking; I'll leave it to thy management.

Engine   I can assure you, if you like the gentleman, the gentleman will like you.

Arabella   Offer no assurances; love is a doubtful voyage.

Engine   Yes, if the venture be in a leaky rotten-bottomed boat such as your husband. But in such a well-built ship, so finely rigged, as that other you speak of, you run no risk at all.

Arabella   Well then go to my Lover and see if he has stowage room left for a heart. If so, contract for mine. But tell him, what foul weather soever happens, he shall preserve my cargo though he throw the rest overboard.

Engine   I have him in sight already; a tall stout vessel, well-manned, bearing up briskly, spreading all sails for haste, and pulling you on board. Methinks I see him lie across your hawser already!

Arabella   Come, wench, thy tongue runs and we lose time.

Engine   I'll regain it on my expedition!

Exeunt.

Scene Two

Ramble's *lodging.*

Enter **Ramble** *and* **Townley**, *in morning gowns.*

Townley   Prethee, Ned Ramble, what makes thee so early a riser, after so late a debauch as we made last night?

Ramble   Business, Frank.

Townley   What business can a Gentleman have to make him rise at ten, that went drunk to bed at four?

Ramble   I am of a mind to pursue an intrigue. A new mistress, Frank.

Townley   An intrigue! I never knew any of your intrigues come to anything.

Ramble   'Tis true, I have been unfortunate hitherto, yet perseverance will overcome destiny.

Townley   Prethee, Ned, I wish you would let women alone and learn to divert thyself with a bottle. Wine is cheaper bought, more easily opened, and quicker dispatched.

Ramble   If I should attend the playhouse once more with you, Frank Townley, and drink as we did yesterday, I should be fit neither for the company of women nor men, I am so squeamish today.

Townley   Custom will overcome that; come let's go and drink away thy complaints.

Ramble   I'll have no more, I thank you, this month.

Townley   But Ned, wine gives a certain elevation of spirit that a man half bowsy shall advance farther with a woman in one encounter, than a sober fellow as thou art in ten. Come, let us abandon this sober end of the Town, where a man can't reel into a Tavern after eleven a'clock, for sawcy Constables that will send him home against his will.

Ramble   Frank, I do decline.

Enter **Roger**.

Roger   Sir, here's a Lady's Maid desires to speak with you in private.

Ramble   Show her in! Did I not tell you, Frank, I had better business today than the bottle?

Townley   A Love Ambassadress?

Ramble   You must doubt it not, but step into the next room.

Townley   I scarce believe thy luck.

Exit **Townley**. *Enter* **Engine**.

Roger   There's my master.

Ramble   A good morrow to you, mistress.

Engine   I wish you the same, sir; and think to bring you such good news my wish will surely be successful.

Ramble   What is it I pray, and from whom?

Engine   From a Fair Lady, sir. Perhaps you will think me forward, should I go on . . .

Ramble   I could never think amiss of one that has such an auspicious countenance.

Engine   You flatter me, I protest I blush at my undertaking.

Ramble   Pray let me hear my fortune from those pretty Lips.

Engine   Sir, consider how accomplish'd a person you are, and how worthily you attract the eyes of the Ladies, and think it then no wonder at all that a certain Lady thinks you the most admirable person of your whole Sex. Since yesterday she spied you at the playhouse . . .

Ramble   At the Playhouse you say, and but yesterday?

Engine   Indeed, sir.

Ramble (*aside*)   Then this is not the invitation I expected.

Engine   My lady talks of you with so much delight and fervency, that I thought it injustice to you, as well as injurious to her, if I should not acquaint you withall, and each with the other.

Ramble   You have rais'd me to a wonderful expectation. Pray who is this Lady?

Engine   A rich Alderman's young wife, one that has been married only Six Months. One that speaks prettily in your praise . . .

Ramble   Good.

Engine   And has the tenderest sentiments in her thoughts for you.

Ramble   Very good.

Engine   And o'er whom you have such an Ascendancy, that could she be assur'd you were one with whom her reputation might be safe . . .

Ramble   She could Love me; is it so?

Engine   It is indeed. After such an assurance, it would not be in her power to refuse you any favour could be expected from a woman.

Ramble   Thou pourest harmony in my ears, that strikes upon my heart-strings, and makes it bound with joy. Take this Gold to encourage thee. Where is this obliging Beauty, when shall I see her?

Engine   Her husband is this day gone out of Town.

Ramble   Conduct me to her.

Engine   Not 'til night, that darkness may secure her reputation. Approach with caution and circumspection, as Misers do the hoard of Wealth they are afraid to lose.

Ramble   I'll think her a Mine of Gold, myself the Indian that has discover'd it, and imagine all other citizens Spaniards that would rob me of't, so secretly I will approach –

Engine   Announce yourself thus . . . (*She knocks the table.*) Such prudence will secure a lasting Joy. This notebook I took from her. Within you will find her name and where she might be found. But interpret not that my errand proceeds from any commands of hers.

Ramble   Not in the least.

Engine   I know the secrets of her heart, and took the liberty without her knowledge.

Ramble   Dear mistress, I am yours.

Engine   Your Servant, sir.

Exit **Engine**. *Enter* **Townley**.

Ramble   Roger! Bring my clothes that I may dress me.

Enter **Roger** *with clothes*.

Townley   Ned, if ever thou prove successful in an intrigue, it will be this.

Ramble   Of that I am inclined to have no doubt. But bless me, Frank, 'tis not the intrigue that I spoke of.

Townley   How say you?

Ramble *shows* **Townley** *a Letter*.

Ramble   This letter I did receive but yesterday.

Townley   A Woman's Hand!

Ramble   And a fair one, I assure you, to send such an invitation. And now I am tempted by another bold Challenger. But twice the chase must yield twice the quarry!

Townley   Are you better acquainted with this first Amour?

Ramble   I have but stood behind her, look'd amorously upon her, and sighed to her across the pew.

Townley   Ah, this is a church Lady then, some rich old widow, for whom thou dost intend with dry slavish lechery to raise thyself to the equipage of a stallion and drudge out a fortune.

Ramble   Have better thoughts, friend; she is neither old nor ugly, nor one whom fortune has yet blessed with widowhood. She is a wife; young, plump, pretty, and blooming as the spring.

Townley   What is her husband?

Ramble   A blockheaded city attorney. A trudging, drudging, curmudgeoning, petitioning citizen, that with a little law, and much knavery has got a great estate.

Townley   A lawyer! Cuckold the Rogue for that reason alone.

Ramble   By the inducement of her parents she married him against her will, and now made nauseous in his bed, rises every morning by six with a pretence to attend church. And loathing his company at home, pretends all day to be at Prayers, that she may be alone in her chamber.

Townley   'Tis strange a man should find a Mistress at Church, that never goes to one.

Ramble   'Tis true: till of late, I had never been at church since my father's funeral, and would not have gone then, but to conduct him thither and ensure he didn't return to take back the Estate I got by his death. Nor had I been since, but for a sudden shower of Rain that drove me inside, where came I by this miracle of a woman, who instantly wrought my conversion.

Townley   And have you said your prayers?

Ramble   I dare not pray against Temptation, lest Heaven should have taken me at my word, and spoil'd my intrigue.

Townley   Spoke like a Cavalier, e'Gad! If thy inclinations did but lie a little more to the Bottle, thou wouldst be an admirably honest Fellow.

Ramble   I must make haste.

Townley   But, Ned, what of the other pretty mackerel circling thy ardent sprat?

Ramble   Curse my luck, that one appointment should prevent the other.

Townley   If you are doubtful, toss a coin.

Ramble   No, I resolve to attempt this one first, because I know the person, and am sure she pleases me. What perfections this one has are yet unknown to me, therefore with more ease is she neglected.

Townley   Who is this morning's woman; what's her name?

Ramble   It is not like a Gallant, to reveal a kind Lady's name. It is here set down in fair characters.

Townley   Let me see that.

Ramble   Look no longer, she's not of your acquaintance.

Townley   Indeed that may be so. The notebook, however, once was mine.

Ramble   Thine! No, thou art deceiv'd.

Townley   Mine. I know it by the Clasps: pray look on the inside of the cover, and see if there be not a cupid drawn with a red-lead pen?

Ramble   Gad, Frank, thou hast guessed right, there is.

Townley   'Tis then the same.

Ramble   Ah.

Townley   The woman I gave it to is the person of all the world I most fancy.

Ramble   Is she very handsome?

Townley   I know not the charms of her face, 'tis her wit I admire.

Ramble   Has your intrigue then been carried on in the dark?

Townley   No, I have seen her often masked at plays. She has a delicate shape, and a pretty hand; she once showed me that as a Sample. Snow was never so white, nor alabaster half so sleek and polished. She is all air, mirth and wit. Roguish, but not impudent. Witty, but not rampant. You should hear her banter most excellently with those cockerels of the pit that come flirting at her. But she always leaves alone when the play is done.

Ramble   But how came she by your notebook?

Townley   But yesterday I was humming a new song in the pit, and she ask'd me if I could give it her. I had it written down, so I presented the book to her. She seemed the most faithful of women, who is revealed the most fickle.

Ramble   I am glad to hear her good character, but am now dissatisfied that one intrigue should cross the other.

Townley   Since it is so, give me the directions, and I will go in your place.

Ramble   Thank you for that, but no. I'll fear not to meet both fair inviters.

Townley   But you can secure only one to yourself.

Ramble   If any accident cross one design, I have the other lady in reserve.

Townley   Thou art ill natur'd, hard-hearted, and wouldst not part with one, hadst thou twenty. For punishment I wish thee the same curse I do to misers that hoard up gold, and would not save a man from starving, which is that you may be robbed of all, and after the loss hang thy self with grief.

Ramble   Alas, Frank Townley, I thought you could not love anything but a Bottle.

Townley   Farewell, churl.

Ramble   In spite of thy prophecy, meet me tomorrow morning, and I'll tell thee such pleasant stories of this night's joys, thou shalt for ever be converted from wine to women.

Women are Miracles the Gods have given.

That by their brightness we may guess at Heaven.

Exeunt.

Act Two

Scene One

A room in **Dashwell***'s house.*

An impressive supper table set. Enter **Eugenia** *and* **Jane**.

Jane   Madam, Mr Ramble awaits at the back door.

Eugenia   Jane, though I love this Mr Ramble, my inclinations are not so much at fault as your counsels. For had not you persuaded me, I should never have consented to his coming. Tonight. In my husband's absence.

Jane   Madam, when a man will press a woman to marry against her inclinations, he lays for himself the foundation of becoming a cuckold shortly after. Troth, madam, think no more of your husband, but of the man you love, who is this night come to your embraces. I'll warrant you you'll not repent tomorrow morning.

Eugenia   If unexpectedly my husband should return –

Jane   There is no fear of that.

Eugenia   Somebody knocks at the front. Run to the door.

Enter **Loveday**, *meanly habited, in black.*

Jane   Who would you speak with, sir?

Loveday   Is Mr Dashwell within?

Jane   He is out of Town.

Eugenia   Jane, who is it?

Jane   A gentleman, madam, to speak to your husband.

Loveday   Madam, I have letters for him from his brother at Hamburg.

Eugenia   Give me the letters, sir. I am sorry for my

husband's absence; our further acquaintance must wait upon
his return.

Loveday   In the letters, madam, your husband's brother
recommends me to him as a servant, and asks that I might be
entertained in this house for a short time. With your
indulgence, madam.

Eugenia   Jane, this is unlucky. What shall we do?

Jane   I could dispatch him to bed, do you but give the order.

Eugenia   Sir, my house is not well provided of beds at
present, you must be content with a lodging in the garret.
Jane, take care to see him lodged, I am sleepy and will go to
my parlour. Jane, make haste, for I am not very well.

Exit **Eugenia**.

Jane   Come, sir, you have rid a long journey today, and
must be weary.

Loveday   I came but from Canterbury today, but must
confess to great hunger!

Jane   Because my Lady's not well, let me beg you be content
with a little cheese tonight, which shall be brought up to you.

Loveday   And a glass of beer at least?

Jane   This is a house of some abstinence. Now, sir, pray
follow me. I shall light your chamber.

Exit **Jane**.

Loveday   How fair Eugenia look'd. With how much joy in
this short interview did I behold those eyes, whose wounds I
have borne so long, whose influence felt at so great a distance!
I wish she had not been indispose'd. What's this? A supper?
Somebody is to come in the husband's absence! Eugenia
pretends to be gone to bed, her indisposition is feign'd, my
company was unseasonable, to lodge me in the Garret was
policy. And so the girl I once knew has indeed become all of a
woman.

Jane (*within*)   Please, sir, come hither.

Loveday   With all my heart, for I am very weary. 'Tis so; they are for posting me supperless to bed, to remove me out of the way. I'll venture to observe.

Exit **Loveday**. *Enter* **Eugenia** *and* **Ramble**.

Eugenia   Come, sir, enter here. Well, Mr Ramble, you see what influence you Gentlemen have over us weak Women.

Ramble   Oh my dear Life, my Joy.

Eugenia   I ne'er thought I should condescend to admit you to my house in my husband's absence thus, what will you think of me?

Ramble   I'll think thee the kindest, loving'st, the dearest, and the best of thy whole sex.

Eugenia   May I then trust, sir, your honour, and intentions?

Ramble   Let me not answer thee, but in this Language.

Eugenia   Jane!

Enter **Jane**.

Jane   Madam?

Eugenia   Is supper upon the Table?

Jane   As you can see, madam.

Eugenia   Come, sir, let us satisfy ourselves with meat and wine.

Ramble   Yet make but a hasty meal of it, that we may the sooner come to that more delicious Banquet, the feast that Love has prepared for us, that feast of Soul and Senses, and of all at once.

Eugenia   Come, sir, now you have said Grace, sit down.

Jane   Less the meat grow cold.

They sit down to Table.

Ramble   Jane, I am obliged to you.

Eugenia   Jane, have a care. Mr Ramble may seek to corrupt you to let him into my chamber after I'm in bed, anon.

Ramble   O sweet wished-for hour!

Eugenia   Be sure, Jane, you don't let him have the key.

Jane   No, madam, I'll be sure to put that in my pocket. When you are both lock'd in.

Ramble   Thank you, Jane.

Exit **Jane**.

Eugenia   I see you have corrupted my Servant already; fie upon you. Come, sir, will you carve?

Ramble   You if you please, madam.

Eugenia   Would you a leg or . . . otherwise? Do not look at me thus, sir; your eyes do tie my tongue.

Ramble   Then let us reserve our thoughts 'til anon, 'til I have thee in bed in my arms, where darkness will privilege thee to tell thy thoughts without a blush freely.

Eugenia   Use your conquest with discretion, and allude not to my blushes. Eat, sir! I confess I can deny you nothing, and 'tis too late now to retreat.

Ramble   Be not faint-hearted, nor ashamed, now Fortune has blessed us with the opportunity. Now let us be all rapture, all fire, kiss, hug, and embrace, and never have done.

Eugenia   Have a care, sir, of feeding too heartily on Love, 'tis a surfeiting diet, with which your sex is soon satisfied. That is the reason you men seek variety so much.

Ramble   Fear not that now, for thou art a dish of all varieties, like tapath. Like a Spanish table that contains the best of everything; all the charms of thy whole Sex are here in this one composition.

Knocking at the door.

Ramble   Who can it be thus late?

Eugenia   Pray Heaven it be not my husband.

Ramble   No no, fortune would not be such an enemy to Love.

Knocking without. Enter **Jane**.

Eugenia   Hark again. Jane! Run to the door and see who knocks.

Jane   I have seen from the window, madam, 'tis my Master!

Eugenia   What shall we do?

Ramble   Cursed spite, where shall I hide?

Jane   Go into the Closet, sir, there, there.

Ramble *goes in. Knocking.*

Eugenia   Heavens, how he knocks. Wait, sir. Thrust in the table and all.

Table and all is put into the Closet.

Eugenia   So, if it be my Husband, tell him I am at my Prayers and would not be disturb'd. Get him up to bed.

Jane   Yes, madam. He'll beat down the door.

Knocking.

Eugenia   Stay, where is my prayer-book?

Jane   In the parlour, madam.

Exit **Jane**. **Eugenia** *settles herself to read upon the couch.*

Enter **Dashwell** *and* **Doodle**, *with* **Jane**.

Dashwell   Jane, you grow slower of service the longer you remain in it. Is my wife in the parlour? We'll go into her.

Jane   She is at Prayers, sir, and would not be disturb'd.

Dashwell   Let her pray anon. . . I have brought Mr

Alderman Doodle to see her. Wife, come prethee. Wife, leave off praying, thou art always a praying, lay by thy book.

Eugenia   Oh me, husband, are you come home, indeed I did not expect you tonight. Mr Alderman, your humble Servant.

Doodle   Your Servant, good Mrs Dashwell.

Eugenia   I hope your wife is well.

Doodle   I left her well in the morning; she's not at her prayers, I'll warrant you, even a little of that suffices her.

Eugenia   Truly I think I cannot better spend my time.

Dashwell   Well, wife, prithee, what hast thou for our supper, we are very hungry, the fresh air has got us a stomach.

Eugenia   Truly, husband, not expecting you home, I provided nothing, we made shift with what was left at dinner, there is nothing at all in the house.

Enter **Loveday**, *with a Letter*.

Dashwell   Who is this?

Eugenia   O my dear, I had forgot to tell you, this young man comes from your Brother with recommendations to you.

Loveday   Here's a letter from him, sir. I was just going to bed, but when I heard you come, I slip'd on my clothes and made bold to know your pleasure.

Dashwell   Indeed, sir. Reach me a Candle from the closet, Jane.

Eugenia   Lord, husband, is it not a little late for business?

Dashwell   Jane, a candle!

Eugenia   How did it happen pray, that you all return'd tonight?

Doodle   Our Brother Alderman heard of a business at the Exchange today, which will require his presence there tomorrow, therefore he resolv'd to bring his Bride to Town tonight, and be Married early in the morning.

Eugenia   Is she come then?

Dashwell   We left her and her Aunt at the Coach-house.

Eugenia   The Marriage I suppose will be private? –

Doodle   Yes, there will be only the Aunt, your husband, and myself. Alderman Wiseacres has the oddest humours; he will have her call him Uncle.

Eugenia   She is very young, I hear.

Dashwell   My Brother gives you a very good character. I'll attempt tomorrow to gain you employment.

Loveday   I humbly thank you, sir.

Dashwell   He names nothing particular; pray what are you capable of?

Loveday   I have been bred a scholar, taken some degrees at the University. Indeed, whilst I was at Oxford, I studied a very Mysterious Art; and spent much time in the contemplation of Magick, which the vulgar call the Black-Art. For this I was expell'd. I can perform wonderful things, yet without danger. Any time when you and your Lady are at leisure, I will show something of my skill for your diversion.

Eugenia   Oh goodness, Husband! I would not see conjuring for all the world, it is a naughty wicked thing, and dangerous.

Loveday   Nay good Lady, you shall have no hurt from me. It is very useful sometimes. I can by my art reveal robberies, procure a wind for ships becalm'd and bring 'em to port, discover private enemies, and the like.

Dashwell   I beg your pardon, I believe nothing of all this.

Doodle   I would you could help us to a good supper, for I am damnably hungry.

Dashwell   Ay, with all the trimmings.

Loveday   That, sir. . . I'll do with all my heart.

Dashwell   Canst thou?

Loveday   In a trice, the easiest thing of a hundred.

Dashwell   Prethee do then.

Eugenia   O Lord husband! What do you mean?

Dashwell   Nay, nay, ne'er fright yourself. You'll see no such thing.

Loveday   I'll warrant you a Supper, sir.

Dashwell   Sayest you so. But let it be hot.

Loveday   Hot. Ay, sir . . .

Doodle   It must needs be hot if it comes from the Devil.

Jane   What does this fellow mean?

Eugenia   I hope he's not in earnest.

Loveday   Fear not, madam, but sit you down; and you, Sir, by your Lady.

Eugenia   For Heaven's sake, husband, let me be gone.

Dashwell   No, no, sit down; let us see it. Begin.

Loveday   Have patience, you shall see nothing to fright you. Silence I pray. Mephorbus, Mephorbus, Mephorbus. Thrice I have thee invoked my Familiar. Be thou assistant to my desires, supply what e'er a hungry appetite requires. By all the powers of the Zodiac, Aries, Taurus, Gemini, Cancer, Leo, Virgo, Libra, Scorpio, Sagittarius, Capricorn, Aquarius, Pisces. Assist ye Seven Planets too, Mars, Sol, Venus, Mercury, Luna, Dragon's Head, and Dragon's Tail. Shed your auspicious influences, and to my charm give efficacious strength.

Jane   Oh the Devil is coming, I smell Brimstone already.

Dashwell   Peace, you Baggage, you've already supped.

Doodle   Would I were under the Table, that the Devil mayn't see me. If he comes.

Loveday   Tacet . . .

Dashwell   That's hold your peace.

Loveday   Arom Gascodin Adelphon, Eus, Eusticon Olam
amemnos.

*After the charms, he stands with his Head as listening to an
invisible.*

Thanks, Mephorbus. Now, sir, you may prepare to tuck in.

Dashwell   Why, I see no meat. The Devil has failed you.

Doodle   I thought you could Conjure.

Loveday   Let your Servant open that door. . . and draw
in the Table as it has been furnished by the Power of
my Art.

Dashwell   As he commands, Jane. Do so.

Jane *opens the closet, draws out the Table.*

Dashwell   Ha! But 'tis wonderful, a table plentifully
furnish'd! Sir, you impress me indeed. Good meat and wine;
'tis excellent. Wife, Mr Alderman, fall to.

Eugenia   Eat of the Devil's food?

Doodle   I warrant you 'tis but a Vision, 'twill vanish if you
touch it.

Loveday   No, though it came by a supernatural means, yet
it is no delusion; 'tis good substantial food, such as nature and
the bounty of Heaven afford. To encourage you, see I will fall
to and eat heartily.

Dashwell   Excellent fare, in faith. O rare Art; sir, you are
an excellent caterer.

Eugenia   I could not have believed there was such power in
Art, if my eyes had not seen it.

Doodle   Pray Heaven it digest well.

Loveday   I warrant you, sir.

Dashwell   Here, sir. Here's to you, and I thank you for our good cheer.

Loveday   Your Servant, sir. Come, Mr Alderman; the cook's good health.

Doodle   Auh! What mean you, drink the Devil's health?

Loveday   Will you eat of his meat and not thank him?

Doodle   'Tis somewhat uncivil, I confess.

Loveday   If you eat with a Tory, the money that bought his meat was the price of orphans' tears, and so came from the Devil too. And yet we eat with him, drink his health, and thank him.

Doodle   Ay, well. . .

Dashwell   If you can do this all the year round, I'll take you to be my book-keeper.

Loveday   My Art serves me only in time of extremity. If done for covetousness, my invocations have no strength.

Dashwell   That's a pity.

Doodle   Pray tell me, by what means was this table furnish'd; was it by the help of Spirits? I heard no noise.

Loveday   It was done by a Familiar that I have command of.

Doodle   Ah.

Loveday   If you please I will shew him in human shape.

Doodle   Oh, no.

Dashwell   Pray do, sir, that I may thank him.

Eugenia   O by no means, sir. What, husband, would you thank the Devil?

Dashwell   Why, is't not the proverb, *Give the Devil his due*? Fear not.

Loveday   I warrant you, Lady, it shall be no harm to you; he is hereabouts invisible already.

Eugenia   Oh.

Loveday   Set the door wide open, that his passage may be free.

Dashwell   Quick, Jane.

Loveday   Mephorbus, that lurkest here, put on human shape, and come forth in the likeness of a fine well-dress'd gentleman, such as may please this Lady's eye. Presto, I say . . . be gone!

Enter **Ramble**.

Loveday   Pass by, pay your reverence, and make your exit.

Ramble *bows and exits.*

Loveday   So, madam, how did you like the Familiar?

Eugenia   It had a frightful shape.

Dashwell   It look'd a fine gentleman.

Doodle   It was a mannerly Devil too, he bow'd as he pass'd by.

Eugenia   Hang a light outside the door to ensure the Devil does not return.

Exit **Jane**.

Dashwell   But pray, why was the door opened, could he not have gone through the keyhole?

Loveday   Yes, sir, but then he would have carried away part of your house; for Spirits are sullen and malicious.

Dashwell   I understand.

Doodle   Well, Mr Dashwell, I'll take my leave.

Dashwell   I'll to the door with you.

Doodle   Mr Conjurer, good night. I thank you for my good supper.

Loveday   Your servant, sir.

Doodle   Madam.

Dashwell *goes out with* **Doodle**. *Enter* **Jane**.

Loveday   Madam, I had not thought so familiar a Familiar would have frighted you.

Eugenia   Jane, help the Gentleman to a Candle.

Jane   Sir, will you please to take that?

Loveday   Madam . . .

Eugenia   Good night, sir.

Dashwell *returns*.

Loveday Good night, sir.

Dashwell   And a good repose to you, sir.

Loveday   Good night, madam.

Exit **Loveday**.

Dashwell   An admirable fellow this, wife.

Eugenia   Oh fie, a wicked man to conjure, and to raise a Devil.

Dashwell   A kind of Devil, but a gentle kind. Come, prethee let's go to bed now.

Eugenia   I could not sleep tonight without saying my prayers again. I have a prayer they say will make evil things fly from one. I'll make use of it tonight.

Dashwell   Should the Spirit return and reveal a devilish nature I'll warrant, wife, you're devout enough to lay him.

Eugenia   I'll say my prayers here below, then I won't disturb you.

Dashwell   Good night then, wife.

Exit **Dashwell**.

Eugenia   Good night. Jane, does Mr Ramble remain hereabout?

Jane   He hovers near the door. He begs you to contrive his admittance for one quarter of an hour.

Eugenia   Go you up, and give me notice when your Master is in bed. When he sleeps we shall once again consider Mr Ramble's suit.

Jane   Yes, madam.

Exit **Jane**.

Eugenia   That silly men conspire to deny each other what the other each doth sorely covet shall not deter me from *my* pleasure. I am now confirmed in my desire to bring this intrigue to a propitious conclusion.

Scene Two

The street, before the houses of **Wiseacres**, **Dashwell** *and* **Doodle**.

Enter **Ramble** *in the street*.

Ramble   Well, here was a defeat of Fortune. I would tempt her once more, but think I shall see what luck I could have with my other Mistress. Indeed, I am confirmed in my pursuit.

Exit **Ramble**. *Enter* **Aunt**, **Peggy** *and a* **Lamp Boy**. *Enter* **Ramble**.

Peggy   Forsooth, Aunt, this is a most hugeous great place.

Ramble   Who goes yonder? Gad, a most pretty creature.

Peggy   Here be a number of houses, Aunt.

Aunt   Ay, Peggy, and fine houses, when you see 'em by daylight.

Peggy   Then shall I see them all tomorrow?

Aunt   O you can't see all London in a week.

Peggy   O Leminy! Not in a week, Aunt?

Ramble   A Country Girl.

Peggy   And does my Nuncle own all the town?

Aunt   All, Peggy? No, nor the King, God bless him, not half.

Ramble   She is so pretty, I cannot forbear speaking to her. By your leave, old Gentlewoman. . .

Aunt   How now, sir, who are you?

Ramble   A Gentleman, and one that desires to be acquainted with you and this little Lady here.

Aunt   Stand off, come away, child, don't let him be near thee.

Ramble   Nay, I'll not part with this pretty hand yet.

Aunt   Shove him away, Peggy.

Peggy   O, but forsooth, Aunt, he's a Gentleman.

Aunt   Ay, but a London Gentleman. Come from him, or he'll bite thee.

Peggy   Deeds, sir, will you bite me?

Ramble   Bite thee! Not for a thousand Worlds. Yet methinks I could eat thee.

Aunt   Stand off, I say, stand off, come away, child, or he'll devour thee.

Ramble   Believe her not, she's a lying envious old woman. I would hug thee, kiss thee, give thee Gold and jewels, make thee a little Queen, if I had thee.

Peggy   O dear Aunt! Did you ever hear the like?

Aunt   Believe him not, he's a lying flattering London Varlet . . . he'll spirit thee away beyond the Sea.

Peggy   Oh la! I won't go beyond the Sea. Oh la, la!

Ramble   Thou shalt not, dear creature, be not afraid. Good Gentlewoman, do not fright a young innocent thing thus . . . I intend her no harm.

Peggy   See you there now, Aunt.

Ramble   I only offer my service to wait on you to your Lodgings.

Aunt   No, sir, let go her hand, we have not so far home, but we can go without your help. Get you gone I say.

Peggy   Nay pray, Aunt, don't beat the Gentleman, he does me no hurt, he only squeezes my hand a little.

Ramble   Oh!

Peggy   Sir, what ails thee?

Ramble   Thy innocence has jarred my heart.

Peggy   Indeed I have not done you no harm, not I?

Ramble   Thou art insensible of the wound thy eyes have made.

Peggy   Wound! Oh dear. Where do you bleed?

Ramble   Oh, 'tis inwardly!

Peggy   Aunt, I warrant you one of your pins has scratched him.

Aunt   Break from him, or he'll bewitch thee.

Enter **Wiseacres** *and* **Doodle**.

Wiseacres   I wonder they are not yet come.

Aunt   Yonder comes your Uncle. Odds me, he'll knock us all on the head. Come away, come away.

Ramble   Hau, let me kiss thy hand first; to part from thee is death.

Wiseacres   Hau! What do I see?

Ramble   Adieu, sweet Innocence.

Wiseacres   Men already buzzing about her, how comes this?

Doodle   Where there is meat in summer, there will be flies.

Wiseacres   I say how comes this?

Ramble   I'll step aside and watch where they go.

Aunt   This rude Royster here would stop us in the street whether we would or no.

Ramble (*aside*)   O you old Crony.

Peggy   Don't make my Nuncle angry, Aunt. He did but hold me by the hand.

Wiseacres   How? Let a man touch you? Did not I warn you not to let any man speak to you?

Peggy   Oh, but he was a Gentleman, and my Aunt told me I must make a curtsy to gentlefolks.

Wiseacres   This was a villain! He would have murther'd thee, and eat thee.

Peggy   Oh grievous! I am glad you came then, Nuncle, he said indeed he could eat me.

Wiseacres   O Monstrous!

Doodle   Be not so passionate; she could not help it.

Wiseacres   I must seem angry to make her afraid for the future.

Aunt   In London they get young folks and bake 'em in Pies.

Peggy   O sadness!

Doodle   What will this come to? Never did I see one so simple.

Wiseacres   What made you stay so long?

Aunt   It was so late we could not get a coach in Southwark, and were forc'd to come on foot.

Peggy   Oh, Nuncle, we came over a bridge where there's a huge pond.

Wiseacres   Lamp Boy, here's sixpence for you, put out your Light and go your ways.

Lamp Boy   Yes, Master.

Exit.

Wiseacres   Alderman Doodle, lead on. Peggy, come give me your hand, Peggy. Here . . . this way . . . so, so, get you in, get you in.

Exeunt as into **Wiseacres'** *house; he shuts the door.*

Ramble   The crafty Old Fox, he put out the lamp that I might not see where they went in. No mind; I have other skillets warming elsewhere if I can now but find my man Roger.

Exit **Ramble**. *Enter* **Townley**.

Townley   Ha, the Light's gone, and I can see nobody! Sure, 'twas Ramble I saw from the Tavern window; he's upon the scent of some new intrigue. If I could have met the Rogue, he should not have scap'd from me till he had drank his bottle. Hark, I hear a door open! It may be him bolting out of some little Cunny-burrough . . .

Enter **Jane**.

Jane   Sir?

Townley   Where is he?

Jane   Sir, you must whisper, for fear of being heard.

Townley   You resolve to determine the way is clear, I'll warrant.

Jane   Sir, where are you?.

Townley   Does the rascal skulk behind you?

Jane   No, sir. He is in bed.

Townley   God rest him!

Take hands.

Jane   My Lady bid me bring you in.

Townley   How say you?

Jane   Having dispatched him upstairs she has a mind now to your company.

Townley Does she?

Jane She sits upon the Couch in the dark, she'll have no light in the room.

Townley Apt modesty indeed.

Jane You must not stay long; therefore what you do, do quickly. Give me your hand.

Townley Yes, but . . .

Jane My mistress awaits, aroused by this night's unfolding all but beyond the bounds of decency.

Townley Then I'll endeavour.

Jane Come, sir, softly.

Townley Here's a blind bargain struck up, but I cannot resist the temptation.

Exeunt, as into **Dashwell**'s *house. Enter* **Ramble** *and* **Roger**.

Roger This, sir, is Alderman Doodle's house. I ask'd three or four innkeepers . . .

Ramble Ha! A neighbourly intrigue! I have a signal that shall open this portal and conduct me to the mortal paradise within.

He knocks.

Ramble Stand there at a distance and wait upon my coming forth.

Arabella *opens the door.*

Ramble Madam?

Arabella Who are you, sir?

Ramble He whose heart has flown before him. Madam, do you see the stars?

Arabella The stars?

Ramble For each we see a thousand more unseen and

none to touch thy beauty, and each and every one conspires to bring us to a sweet embrace.

Arabella *closes the door.*

Ramble   Roger, you are sure you have not mistaken the House?

Roger   Ay, sir, there's no other great green door but that. They all told me at the great green door.

Ramble   Dolt! I seek an ocean of delight and you tangle us in a shallow backwater. Walk on and discover this Doodle's true abode!

Exeunt **Ramble** *and* **Roger**. *Enter* **Engine** *and* **Arabella**.

Engine   Indeed, he is the same man to whom I gave your token, and is known as Mr Ramble.

Arabella   And there is your mistake; for you thought I meant Ramble, when I ask'd who Townley was!

Engine   They are constant Companions, madam. And were then together at the Play.

Arabella   You must haste to tell him 'tis a mistake, and that he is not the person I did expect.

Engine   O, madam, by no means, lest for revenge he should discover to your husband!

Arabella   Do you think he would do so ill a thing?

Engine   Who knows how he may resent the disappointment; 'twould be such an affront you must suppose the worst.

Arabella   They are returned; make haste.

Exeunt **Arabella** *and* **Engine**. *Enter* **Ramble** *and* **Roger**.

Ramble   The Devil take this night; there is no other door it can be but this. My good friend Townley did assert this lady's fickle nature. But here is one could be trusted with thy heart. The door is fast. To knock is not convenient, to expect is painful, but a Lover must have patience, a little sufferance sweetens the delight. My trust is still in faithful Eugenia.

Jane *opens the door. Enter* **Townley** *and* **Eugenia**, *embracing.*

Jane   Step this way, sir, and swiftly.

Ramble   What is this?

Jane   Come, madam, do not detain him any longer, 'tis dangerous.

Eugenia   Yet is it not unmannerly that one should go so soon, that did come so suddenly?

Ramble   Hau!

Townley   Dear kind sweet creature, when shall I be thus bless'd again?

Eugenia   Often, if you be discreet.

Townley   I could live an Age in thy arms, this was so very short –

Eugenia   Ere long, we'll find whole hours of pleasure. Of all men, sir, it is you and you alone who . . . who in God's Heaven are you, sir?

Ramble   Have at thee, traitor; draw, and fight.

He draws, and runs at **Townley**. **Eugenia** *and* **Jane** *run in, and close the door.*

Eugenia/Jane   Ah, ah, ah!

Roger   Hold, hold, Master, hold, 'tis Mr Townley, 'tis Mr Townley.

Ramble   Ha, Townley.

Townley   Ramble! What a plague did you mean?

Ramble   To have kill'd you, had you not been my very good friend.

Townley   Short warning, prethee next time give me leave to make my Will.

Ramble   How came you here?

Townley   By the wheel of fortune, I can scarcely tell thee.
Prethee, who was this Wench, with whom I have had so sweet
a satisfaction?

Ramble   I perceive your innocence by warrant of your
ignorance. 'Twas one of my two intrigues. I beat the bush, but
thou has catch'd the bird.

Townley   Ned, I only took a potshot. And my aim was
untrue. Next time she'll be your game.

Ramble   A curse on all ill luck.

Townley   I told you in the morning, fortune would jilt you.
Come, walk off; I have company staying for me at the Tavern.

Ramble   Fortune is the wind and woman the tide; both turn
all ways to confound the steadfast voyager. I shall in future
make more haste and be not easily put off.

Exeunt.

Act Three

Scene One

A room in **Doodle**'s *house.*

Enter **Arabella** *and* **Engine**.

Arabella   Engine; you have discovered him?

Engine   On the steps of the Tavern, madam, and I have summoned him.

Arabella   Is there no other remedy to keeping his counsel?

Engine   None but the simplest, madam.

Arabella   Indeed, I have no aversion to his person. And if I had never seen that Townley, I should have somewhat liked this Ramble.

Engine   Resolve to go forward now, you'll like him better tomorrow morning, I warrant you.

Arabella   Well, if he press very hard, and I find I cannot otherwise make sure of him . . .

A knock at the door, opened by **Engine**. *Enter* **Ramble**.

Ramble   Madam.

Arabella   I thank you, sir, for returning, and would beg your understanding. My rude dismissal of your tender suit being but the modest constraint of one unused to such endeavours.

Ramble   Such discretion only serves to sweeten the dish. And one that is long in preparation commands an even greater appetite.

Arabella   Your meaning escapes me, sir.

Ramble   I mean to enquire, madam, why you are not yet in bed?

Arabella   Is it late, sir?

Ramble   Oh very late; and sitting up is pernicious to beauty . . .

Arabella   I have but little, and should preserve it. In order therefore to do so, sir, I beg your pardon, and take my leave.

Ramble   Ay to bed, to bed. Miss Engine, pray help me disrobe.

Arabella   What mean you, sir?

Ramble   Faith, to go to bed too . . .

Arabella   You'll go home first?

Ramble   Devil take me if I do. I mean to stay and sleep with you.

Arabella   With me?

Ramble   Even so.

Arabella   Whether I will or no?

Ramble   That's e'en as you please; if you are as willing as I, 'tis so much the better.

Arabella   Sure you are but in jest.

Ramble   Come, madam, I know how matters go; you are a fine, brisk, handsome Lady, and have a dull dronish husband without a sting; I am a young active fellow fit for employment, and e'Gad I know your wants. Therefore, madam, come. Your nightdress becomes you so well, and you look so very tempting . . . I can hardly forbear you a minute longer.

Arabella   I should chide you severely now, for your ill opinion of me, but I perceive you are beyond saving.

Ramble   I am not so stiff-necked a Sinner but I may be mollified by morning.

Arabella   No, I am very sleepy and must go to bed, therefore pray be gone.

Ramble If I go tonight, I do deserve to be canonis'd!

Arabella Sir, if you do hope . . .

Ramble I have all hope, and faith, and charity. Hope that you love me, faith to believe you dissemble, and Charity enough to supply your wants in your husband's absence.

Arabella Sir, I find you intend to be troublesome. I shall leave you.

Ramble But I shan't leave you.

Arabella Why, what do you intend to do?

Ramble To follow you.

Arabella Whither?

Ramble To your Chamber.

Arabella For what?

Ramble To hug, kiss, and come to bed with you.

Arabella You would not dare it.

Ramble So I would.

Arabella Since you are so resolute, I'll shall indeed retire.

Ramble Perhaps you'll lock the door.

Arabella I scorn to do so. I'll see what you dare do.

Ramble I'll dare if I die for't.

Arabella Take notice then, thou desperate resolute man, that I now go to my chamber, where I'll undress me, go into my bed, and if you dare to follow me, kiss, or come to bed to me; if all the strength and passion a provoked Woman has, can do't, I'll lay thee breathless and panting, and so maul thee, thou shalt ever after be afraid to look a woman in the face.

Ramble Stay and hear me now: Thou shalt no sooner be there but I'll be there; kiss you, hug you, down with you, and as often as I down with you, be sure to give you the rising-blow, that if at last you do chance to maul me, 'Gad you shan't have much reason to brag in the morning. And so angry, threatening woman, get thee gone and do thy worst.

Arabella   And you, sir, do you your best. Adieu.

Exit **Arabella**.

Engine   Well here is like to be fearful doings. Here's heavy threatening on both sides.

Ramble   I long till the skirmish begins.

Engine   Pray, sir, do not tarry; she has nothing but her nightgown to slip off.

Ramble   I shall have her at my mercy. Think you she consents?

Engine   Oh, sir, have no mercy on her, she'll not complain of hard usage, I warrant you.

Ramble   Then, to the fray!

Exit **Ramble**.

Engine   Let me see, what has my pain-taking brought me in since morning. One–two–three–four guineas. This is a profitable profession. This employment was formerly named bawding and pimping, but our Age is more civilis'd and our Language much refin'd. It is now called doing a friend a favour. Whore is now prettily call'd Mistress. Pimp; friend. Cuckold-maker; gallant. Thus the terms being civilis'd the thing itself becomes more acceptable. What Clowns they were in former Ages.

Enter **Doodle**.

Doodle   Where are you here?

Engine   Ha! My Master.

Engine *runs to the chamber door and seems to speak as rejoicing.*

Engine   O Lord, madam, here's my Master, here's my Master, here's my Master, my Master's come . . .

Doodle   Why are the doors open at this time of night?

Engine   My Master, madam, my Master's come, O
lemminy.

Doodle   Well?

Engine   My Master. My Master.

Doodle   Are you mad? I say why were the doors left open
thus late?

Engine   I was standing at the door, and my Lady called all
of a sudden. I am so glad you are come home, Master.
Madam, here's my Master. My Master's here!

Doodle   Rogues might have come in and rob'd the house.

Engine   Indeed, sir! Madam; my Master's home.

Enter **Arabella** *in nightgown and slippers, runs and hugs him about
the neck.*

Arabella   Oh my dear. Dear . . . dear. Art thou return'd?

Doodle   I have been come to Town a great while.

Arabella   Oh my dear, dear. . . dear dear.

Engine   Hist.

Beckons to **Ramble** *to slip by – he comes stealing out.* **Doodle** *turns
and he slips back again.*

Doodle   Yes, wife, but I am very sleepy and must retire.

Arabella   Oh, you are a naughty hubby. You have been a
great while in Town, and would not come home to me before.
I won't love you now I think on't.

Doodle   I'll be going to bed then.

Arabella   Ay, but you shall kiss me first, your constant wife.

She hugs him again, **Engine** *beckons to* **Ramble**, *who comes out but
retreats.*

Kiss me. Kiss me heartily.

Doodle   So, so, wife. Prethee be quiet.

Arabella   Oh my hubby, dear, dear, dear hubby . . .

Engine   Hem – em . . . ah . . .

Ramble *comes out and retreats again.*

Doodle   I am so weary, and thou stand'st hugging me . . .

Arabella   Well, we shall remember this. You are come home and will make no fuss of me.

Doodle   Prethee, let me go to bed.

Arabella   Engine, let us go see what's in the house for your Master to eat.

Doodle   I have supp'd already, wife.

Arabella   And what had my dear for supper –

Doodle   A few oysters, and a young Partridge.

Arabella   And how far went dear today?

Doodle   A few Miles . . .

Arabella   And what time came you back?

Doodle   Prethee, wife, why stand'st thou asking me so many questions.

Arabella   Untie your Master's shoes the while –

Doodle   No no, leave your fussing, give me my Cap and Nightgown.

Arabella   Engine, run into the Chamber and fetch 'em.

Doodle   No matter, we'll go in . . .

Exit **Engine**. **Arabella** *sings.*

Arabella   I have a husband, but what of that?
  He neither loves me . . . nor my . . . little pussy Cat;
  Little Pussy gets a Mouse and with it does play.
  But my husband ignores me all the long day –

Doodle   Prethee, wife, do not be so troublesome.

Arabella   There was a Lady lov'd a Swine, quoth she.
Dear Pig-hog quoth she, wilt thou be mine? . . .
Hunh! quoth he . . . diddly di.
Husband, you lov'd to see me merry formerly.

Doodle   Yes, wife, but I am so sleepy tonight.

Enter **Engine**.

Engine   Sir, there's none of your gown in the Chamber.

Doodle   Stay, now I think on't, 'tis in my Counting-house.
Go to bed, wife, I'll undress me there, and come to you.

Arabella   There were some letters come today; you should
perhaps look over them.

Doodle   No, no, I'll come presently . . .

Exit **Doodle**.

Arabella   Fox! Come out of your hole. Make haste, lest he
returns.

Enter **Ramble**.

Engine   Madam, the door; my Master has locked it, and
taken out the key.

Ramble   Then which way shall I get out?

Arabella   Ah ha ha . . .

Ramble   Is all this a laughing matter?

Arabella   I laugh at your faint heart . . .

Engine   What shall we do, madam?

Arabella   You must take Mr Ramble into your chamber,
and let him sleep in your bed.

Ramble   What, within there?

Arabella   Even so, sir.

Engine   And thank your Stars.

Ramble   'Gad I sweat with the thought of it.

Engine   And well may you, sir, for my Mistress is given to walk in her sleep. And if in the middle of the night she should chance to come to your bedside, and take you betwixt sleeping and waking . . .

Ramble   Say, madam, would you be so kind?

Engine   That may easily be. My Master will soon be asleep, as you may know by his snoring.

Ramble   But, should he wake, and miss her?

Arabella   To prevent that danger, Engine, come you to my bedside. Softly, I'll rise, and you shall lie down in my place.

Engine   Methinks in this endeavour I am become a little too involved. What, madam, if my master awake and turn to me?

Arabella   He'll find thee a Woman, will he not?

Engine   Nay, now with your leave . . .

Ramble *gives her money.*

Engine   Rather than spoil a good intrigue, I'll venture.

Arabella   An excellent device.

Engine   Get you both in.

Arabella   This is likely such an unlucky project, I would not venture but that the very thought of it now demands its consummation.

Engine   Go, go, my Master's coming back.

Exeunt **Arabella** *and* **Ramble**. *Enter* **Doodle**, *in a cap and nightgown.*

Doodle   Is my wife in bed?

Engine   Softly, sir, she's asleep.

Doodle   So, so, good night, make haste to bed.

Exit.

Engine   Oh the vain imaginations of a husband, who thinks

himself secure of a wife! I long to be married to show my wit.
Indeed there is no distance between man and woman that the
other will not cross; he crowing all the while, she travelling
silent. My Master snores already. Now must I lie by that dull
drowsy animal.

Enter **Arabella** *in her nightgown.*

Arabella   Softly, wench, softly . . .

Engine   I warrant you, madam . . . he snores like a Turk.

Arabella   Have a care of waking him.

Engine   You instruct me in mine own strict intention,
madam. Have you a care to make good use of your time, and
don't stay too long.

Exit **Arabella**.

Engine   So. Thus far all goes well. Now must I undergo the
severe penance, to lie by a man and sweating for fear he
should wake, and find me out. Or to the worse; wake and find
me to his liking. But I must venture now, so happy go lucky
and to bed go I.

Roger (*without*)   Fire! Fire Fire!

Engine   Hark!

Knocking at the door.

Roger (*without*)   Fire! Fire . . . Fire . . .

Engine   O Heavens . . . we are undone . . . they cry Fire!

Enter **Arabella**.

Arabella   O, Engine, don't you hear 'em knock, and cry
fire!

Roger (*without*)   Fire, fire, fire!

Arabella   This will certainly waken him anon. Let us cry
fire too, and say, I am just got up. Fire. Fire. Fire . . .

Roger (*without*)   Fire, fire, fire.

Engine   Fire. Fire. Fire.

Enter **Ramble**.

Ramble   Fire. Fi . . . !

Arabella/Engine   Hist!

Ramble   What must I do now?

Engine   Don't stir out till my Master's gone.

Exit **Ramble**. *Enter* **Doodle**.

Doodle   What's the matter, is the house on fire?

Engine   Don't you hear 'em knock?

Doodle   Open the door.

Engine   Give me the Key.

Doodle   Follow me. All follow me! Oh fire . . . fire . . . fire . . .

Exeunt **Arabella**, **Engine**, **Doodle**. *Enter* **Ramble**.

Ramble   What must I do now, venture to be discover'd, or stay here and die a martyr to save a Lady's honour? A pox of luck still. My life or her good name? It takes but small consideration.

Enter **Engine**.

Engine   Here is no smell of burning, nor any smoke. Be you mad? Hide thyself! Sure the fire is not in this house.

Ramble *hides beneath her skirts. Enter* **Doodle** *and* **Arabella**.

Doodle   Why, here's no fire, nor nothing like it. Come, wife . . . come in again. They knock, and cry fire, as if they were mad, and yet there was nobody!

Arabella   It was a false Alarm.

Doodle   This was the roguery of some drunken fellows in their night frolics.

Arabella   I am glad it was no worse.

Doodle   Mistress Engine, pray lock the doors.

Engine   Yes, sir.

Doodle   Pray then, do so.

Engine   Now, sir?

Doodle   At once.

Engine   Deeds, sir, I would not.

Doodle   How say you?

Engine   It does not take my fancy.

Arabella   Engine, do as thy master would instruct.

Engine   Indeed, madam, I would do whatever you will, were it not beneath me.

Doodle   You dare to reveal thy cheek in such abundance?

Engine   'Tis not my choice to do so, sure.

Arabella   Engine, what has got into you?

Engine   Nothing, madam, though 'twould not be my choice neither.

Doodle   Plague on thy disrespect; I say you; lock the doors.

He thrusts her to the door, revealing **Ramble**.

Arabella   Husband, I swoon.

Doodle   Say you so?

Arabella   These cries of fire and sudden comings to and going fro have quite upset my humour. I do faint.

Doodle   Indeed I fear so.

Ramble *sneaks out of the door.* **Engine** *closes it.*

Engine   There, sir, I have locked the door. Here is your key, sir. The door is locked. As you did request me, so indeed the door is most securely locked.

Doodle   Well, well . . .

Engine   As you did request me to lock the door, sir, so have
I . . .

Doodle   Enough. Thy mistress swoons. Bring aqua vitae.

Engine   If you request it, sir, so it shall be done.

Doodle   Come, wife, to bed.

Exeunt **Doodle** *and* **Arabella**.

Engine   Now this night's intrigues surely must lie beyond
any success.

Scene Two

The street before **Doodle**'s *house*.

Enter **Ramble**.

Ramble   This is scarce worth believing! To come so near to
paradise but twice, deeds but thrice if Mistress Engine had
never locked her door. There is but little now left of this night
but to return home. Who's there?

Roger   'Tis I, sir. Your man Roger.

Ramble   Did I not send you home?

Roger   I'll tell you, sir, that you may know, what a piece of
service I have done you, and how fitly qualified am I to be
your servant.

Ramble   Well, sir, in what?

Roger   I guessed, sir, by your sending me home, that your
intention was to lay a better game than cards tonight, and
'twas a lucky thought, for you were no sooner indoors but I
perceived a man come plodding along, go in without
knocking, and shut the door. So this, thought I, is the
husband. And now thought I must my master be thrust into a
closet and remain in purgatory all night . . . unless I work his
deliverance.

Ramble   And so, sir?

Roger   So I cried out fire. And thundered and knocked 'til I raised the house and put the people in confusion that you might escape in the hurry. Now, sir, if you will speak your conscience, I do believe this piece of policy did bring you off. Your bare acknowledgement, sir, will be to me above any reward.

Ramble   It was you then that knocked and cried out fire?

Roger   Yes, sir; at your service.

Ramble   Lend me that stick in your hand.

Roger   This stick; for what, sir?

Ramble   Lend it me, I say.

Roger   Here, sir.

Ramble   Now will I reward your excellent piece of service.

Beats him.

Roger   Oh sir; what do you mean, sir?

Ramble   To beat you till you have no invention left!

Roger   Oh, oh oh, sir, will you be ungrateful, sir, will you be ungrateful?

Ramble   It was you, you dog, hindered me of the sweetest enjoyments man ever missed!

Roger   'Twas well meant! Indeed, sir, 'twas well meant!

Ramble   Be gone and come not near me this week, lest I beat thee to pulp!

Exit **Roger**. **Engine** *at the window.*

Engine   Sir. Mr Ramble.

Ramble   Here.

Engine   Spite of all, my Lady is still willing, but my master took the key again.

Ramble   Is there no window to creep in?

Engine   Just there below is a cellar-hole with a bar out. Try if you can get in there.

Ramble   I have found it.

Engine   Try if it be wide enough to get through.

Ramble   I believe it is.

Engine   I'll come down then and open the cellar door.

Ramble   Do. Do, rare creature . . . I'll go heels forward because I don't know how far it is to the bottom. So . . . hup. Hup. This hole begins to grow tighter. Hup. Hup. The reward of lovers has needs be so sweet for which they endure so much. Hup. Hup. 'Tis damnably narrow now, but I'll another squeeze . . . hup, hup hup . . . Oh, my guts. I can't get an inch further. What a spite this is. I'll have to come out again.

Engine *above at the window.*

Engine   Sir, sir . . . where are you?

Ramble   Where are you?

Engine   Here above. The cook has locked the cellar door. If you do get in you can't come upstairs.

Ramble   Then I must give this up for tonight, and think of a stratagem against tomorrow. Hup . . . Hup . . . Hup . . . I can neither get quite in nor out.

Engine   How, sir?

Ramble   I am stuck! Hup-a . . . hup-a . . . hup-a . . . There is some damned hook or staple on the inside has got hold of my clothes.

Engine   Ha ha ha.

Ramble   A pox on this.

Engine   Ha ha ha.

Enter a **Vendor**, *singing, passing by.*

Vendor   'Taters!

Ramble   Yonder comes company; now shall I be taken for a house-breaker.

Engine   'Tis none but a vendor. Be silent and he'll pass you by.

Vendor   'Taters!

As he passes **Ramble**, *stokes his fire, knocking out clinker.*

Vendor   Will you have a 'tater!

Ramble   Ahhh.

Vendor *exits.*

Engine   Sir; what is the matter?

Ramble   Son of a whore! He has thrown his clinker in my face!

Engine   Ha ha ha . . . excuse me, sir, I can't forbear . . . ha ha ha.

Ramble   S'death how it burns!

Engine   Hist, sir. Hist. You will waken the household.

A window opens above, and **Doodle** *throws the contents of a chamber-pot upon his head as he looks up, then retires.*

Ramble   Augh!

Engine   What's the matter, sir?

Ramble   One rogue has set me on fire and another has quenched me with a stale chamberpot. Faugh, how it stinks.

Engine   My master Doodle is regular in habits.

Ramble   Never was a lover in such a pickle!

Engine   Truly, this is enough to cool anybody's courage.

Ramble   Hup-a . . . hup-a . . . hup-a . . . It won't do, I am as fast as if I were wedged in.

Engine   Be silent; here come some others.

Enter two **Chimney-Sweeps**.

1st Chimney-Sweep   Hold, Tom, stay. I am damnably grip'd in my guts. I must unfasten.

2nd Chimney-Sweep   Make haste then.

1st Chimney-Sweep   Oh, I am damnably full of wind.

Stands with back against **Ramble**'s *face and untrusses. (Farts, surely.)*

Ramble   Faugh! Oh, you stinking cur. Away with you.

2nd Chimney-Sweep   Who's there?

Ramble   A friend.

1st Chimney-Sweep   Who are you?

2nd Chimney-Sweep   What are you?

Ramble   A gentleman. Pray help me here for I am stuck fast; lend me your hands.

Engine   'Tis true, friends; help the gentleman out.

1st Chimney-Sweep   Hark you, Tom; a rare opportunity. Take you hold of him by that arm . . . Hold, sir, we shall spoil your hat and periwig . . .

2nd Chimney-Sweep   Give me your sword, sir, that you may not do yourself damage . . .

Ramble   Thank you, sirs.

They take off his hat and periwig, clap one of their sooty hats on his head, blacken his face and run away.

1st Chimney-Sweep   Now, Tom . . . Scour and away!

Ramble   What? Thieves! Thieves!

Engine   What have they done, sir?

Ramble   The rogues are run away with my new beaver hat. And my periwig and sword.

Engine   Oh the rascals . . .

1st Watchman   Watch ho!

Engine   Sir, your crying out has raised the watch; what will you do now?

Ramble   Now? Now I shall be lodged in the jail, carried before a magistrate tomorrow, and talked of in every coffee-house by noon. Then the bards shall make my name a jest over all over the nation!

Enter **Watchmen** *with lanterns.*

1st Watchman   Here; this way they cried thieves! Follow!

2nd Watchman   Ay, 'Twas hereabouts.

3rd Watchman   Ha! Here's one lies upon the ground.

1st Watchman   Are you killed, sir? Speak.

2nd Watchman   Ay; if you are dead, pray tell us.

Ramble   No, friends; I am hardly hurt at all.

3rd Watchman   Hau, neighbours; he is halfway in at the grates. This is some thief!

2nd Watchman   Ay, come to rob the house.

Ramble   Pray help me out, friends, and I'll tell you the truth.

1st Watchman   Hold there; there may be more rogues inside; let us knock and raise the house.

3rd Watchman   Ay; knock hard.

2nd Watchman (*knocks hard at the door*)   Rise. Thieves here, thieves in your house!

Ramble   Now shall I further be disgraced.

Doodle *appears above.*

Doodle   Hold. Hold; are you mad? What's the matter there?

2nd Watchman   We have catched a thief creeping in at your cellar door.

Doodle   A thief!

1st Watchman   We believe there are some other rogues in the house already.

Doodle   Honest Watchmen, I thank you. I'll come down.

Ramble   Pray you honest Watchmen, help me out, for I am in a great deal of pain.

1st Watchman   Come, neighbours; we may venture to pull him out now.

2nd Watchman   Pull you by that arm.

3rd Watchman   Pluck hard!

Ramble   Oh . . . I would I were like an egg steeped in vinegar.

3rd Watchman   Nay; you must endure it.

1st Watchman   Come, neighbours; all hands to the work . . .

Ramble   Zounds, my guts!

2nd Watchman   So, 'tis done. Get up, sir.

Enter **Doodle** *in nightgown with headpiece, bandoleers and a musket charged and cocked.*

Doodle   Come, where is this thief, where are these rogues?

2nd Watchman   We suppose there are some in the cellar, that got in before.

Enter **Arabella** *and* **Engine**.

Doodle   Say you so? Say you so? If there be, I'll send 'em out!

Doodle *shoots the musket off into the cellar, and falls backward as if knocked down.*

Oh, neighbours. Neighbours. Oh.

1st Watchman   You han't hurt yourself, Master, I hope?

Doodle   Is my right arm on?

1st Watchman   Indeed, sir; stir it, sir. Do you feel any pain?

Doodle   No, not at all.

2nd Watchman   Get up then, Master; there's no harm done.

Doodle   Always was a damn obstinate piece.

2nd Watchman   Hold, sir!

Doodle   Is this the rogue?

1st Watchman   Whilst you examine him, we'll search below.

Doodle   Ay, pray do. Engine, go below with the Watchmen.

Exeunt **Engine** *and* **1st Watchman**.

Arabella   What's the matter here, husband?

Doodle   We have catched a thief, wife.

Ramble   Sir, I am a gentleman, and one that scorns such base actions. I'll tell you in short, Sir, how I came to be fastened in your window.

Doodle   Ay that, sir. Do so.

Ramble   . . . Walking down the street for a little air I was dogged by two or three rogues who came up behind me and began to rifle my pockets. Knowing I had this purse of gold about me, slid from them upon the ground, found my feet at the cellar window and crowded myself as far in as I could to secure my pockets.

Doodle   Then you cried out thief yourself?

Ramble   Yes; 'twas I.

Arabella   'Tis very likely, husband.

Doodle   Ay, so 'tis. And if nobody be found in my house, I'll release you.

Enter **Engine** *and* **1st Watchman**.

1st Watchman   We can find nobody, sir.

Engine   We have looked so much as in the oven, and the cistern.

Doodle   Well, sir, your servant then. Watchmen, see this gentleman home.

1st Watchman   What, must he be released?

2nd Watchman   Ay; he's an honest gentleman and has been robbed himself.

Ramble   Sir, good night to you. Your servant, madam.

Arabella   Sir, if your mistress was but here in my place to see you now, she could not choose but to love you for such a piece of gallantry, and take you about the neck, and kiss you.

Ramble   Madam, you are kind.

Arabella   Had you but first washed your face.

Doodle   Pray excuse her, sir; my wife's a merry prating wag . . .

Ramble   I like her ne'er the worse.

Doodle   Good night, sir.

Ramble   Your servant, sir. Good night, madam.

Arabella   Good night, sweep.

Doodle   Come, wife; you are a little too severe with the gentleman.

Arabella   What, should I have no revenge of him for raising us out of our beds?

Exit **Doodle**, **Arabella** *and* **Engine**. *Enter* **Townley** *and* **Tom**.

Ramble   Come, gentlemen, forward to my lodging.

Townley   Now you dog, am not I very merry? This 'tis to be drunk, you dog.

Tom   Sir, don't make such noise. We are near the watch.

Townley   Watch? Shew 'em me, that I may scour among 'em; I ne'er killed a Watchman yet.

1st Watchman   Who goes there?

Townley   You are the son of a whore!

3rd Watchman   Knock him down.

Ramble   No, be kind to him. He is a friend of mine. He's in drink.

Townley   Hold, a truce. Truce. A friend of thine? Who the Devil art thou?

Tom   By his clothes, sir, it should be Mr Ramble.

Townley   Ramble! Pox on't, hold up your light. Ramble! What the pox art thou doing thus, like the Prince of Darkness with these hell-hounds about thee, and in this pickle?

Ramble   Misfortunes, Frank. Misfortunes.

1st Watchman   The gentleman has been knocked down and robbed, sir.

Townley   No, neighbours, this comes of whoring.

Ramble   Hold your tongue.

Townley   And the husband came and you were forced to creep up the chimney to get away. This comes of your whoring still.

3rd Watchman   No, sir, indeed; there's been a burglary.

Townley   Burglary, Ned? Burglary? Worse and worse. This comes of whoring still. Hereafter, Ned, be ruled by me; leave whoring and burglary and fall to honest drinking.

Ramble   Watchmen, prethee go home; this gentleman and I lodge in the same house.

Townley   Look you, friends; I'll go home if you please, but for this wild man here, take a backroom for him at some great inn, hang out his picture, blow a trumpet, and show him for a groat a piece. I warrant you you'll raise a fortune.

1st Watchman   In company you will safely home. We'll go our ways. Good night.

Exeunt the **Watchmen**.

Townley   Well, Ned, to tell the truth, I am a little ashamed of your company at present.

Ramble   I curse my stars.

Townley   'Tis in vain. They will shed their malicious influence.

Ramble   Considering how my supper fell into your mouth earlier, you should thank the stars. I started the hare, gave her the long course, and you took her at the half turn.

Townley   Make your court to the bottle, Ned, to the bottle.

Ramble   I take your council and will forswear all womankind! But for the hope I have to bring one of these two designs to perfection.

Townley   Still wilt thou be mislead by hopes; hope is more flattering than women and less faithful than good fortune.

Ramble   Frank, you speak well. Hope is the whore that breeds all ill-luck. A pox on her, and on womankind also.

Drinks. Enter **Jane**.

Jane   Here's a letter, sir.

Ramble   Ha!

Jane   To be delivered to you with all speed.

Ramble   Let me see it quickly.

Exit **Jane**.

Ramble   From Eugenia!

Townley   Ay, the Devil's come abroad again to hinder your conversion.

Ramble (*reads*)   'Sir, my husband will be from home all tomorrow morning. I am very desirous to be informed of the particulars of last night's misfortune; curiosity forces me, in spite of blushes, to give you this invitation.' Yes!

Townley   Ay, the Devil dances again.

Ramble   Frank, is not here temptation now, is it to be resisted think you? Can flesh and blood forbear going? What can hinder now? Frank Townley, give me thy hand. If I fail now, I will from this time give over assignation and stratagems and be thy convert for ever. Let us go home. Tomorrow's return shall see me victorious!

Interval.

Act Four

Scene One

Communal gardens behind **Wiseacre***'s,* **Doodle***'s and* **Dashwell***'s houses. A gate and summer house.*

Enter **Dashwell** *and* **Doodle***,* a*s from the wedding.*

Dashwell   Are the Bride and the Groom come from the church?

Doodle   Indeed, Mr Alderman. But why do we wait in the gardens?

Dashwell   It is our brother Wiseacres' wish that his coming home with his Bride be no public spectacle, and this rear entry thus becomes his married threshold.

Doodle   'Tis a shorter route also, and more suited to his years. Here come the happy couple.

Enter **Wiseacres***,* **Aunt** *and* **Peggy***, being carried by a* **Coachman***.*

Wiseacres   In, sir; in. Make haste.

Peggy   Indeed, husband, this is a fine transport.

Wiseacres   Over the threshold, sir, deposit her thus. Cover thy head, wife; I would not have thee seen by neighbours all and sundry. Here's money for you, sir.

Coachman   None desired, sir; 'twas a light burden and a pretty one.

Wiseacres   Be gone, Scoundrel. Make thy way.

Exit the **Coachman***,* **Aunt** *and* **Peggy***.*

Dashwell   Methought it a fine ceremony, Mr Alderman, though the chapel be small, and the congregation no greater than could fill a single pew.

Wiseacres   I would not have a public marriage, sir, for all the town to pry and tittle-tattle after.

Doodle   Though our wives are like to protest at their absence.

Wiseacres   Let 'em, Mr Alderman. I would not have the wives in particular; lest they lay claim to friendship of the Bride and turn her head from her husband. Let marriage be man's business, I say.

Dashwell   And will you now be about it, sir?

Wiseacres   What, say you?

Dashwell   Your business, sir.

Wiseacres   Indeed, sir. I am inclined to wait upon it.

Doodle   Such may you be thus compelled, for as we came in at the gate a messenger did give me this; 'tis from the Master of the ship in which we all have great concerns and is come up the river today. He desires us to take a boat and go down this tide.

Wiseacres   No question, we must go.

Dashwell   Methinks it is very unlucky that business should fall out thus on your Wedding day, and force you to leave your Bride unbedded.

Wiseacres   Indeed, but business is more pressing. I shall never be much concerned at anything that calls me away, knowing what security I have of my wife in her simplicity.

Doodle   So you have said, sir, but I shall not be converted without a Miracle.

Wiseacres   We have time afore the tide; I will now shew you an example that shall convince you of your error. Ho, Wife . . . Peggy . . . Pray sit and observe; you shall behold and wonder.

Enter **Aunt** *and* **Peggy**.

Aunt   Here, and please you is your Bride . . .

Wiseacres   There's my dainty Peggy. Peggy. Come to me, Peggy.

Peggy   Yes forsooth.

Wiseacres   And pray, Aunt; fetch me from the house the fine gilt cap and halberd that stands in the hall. And my nightcap, also.

Aunt   If you will, sir. Peggy, where's your Curtesie to your Nuncle and the Gentlemen?

Exit **Aunt**.

Wiseacres   Indeed; your Curtesie . . .

Peggy *curtsies*.

Wiseacres   So, that's as I am your Uncle; another now as I am your husband . . . So, now stand before me. You know, Peggy, you are now my wife.

Peggy   Yes forsooth, so Naunt tells me.

Wiseacres   And that is a happiness for which you are to thank Heaven, that you have married a discreet sober person.

Peggy   Yes forsooth.

Wiseacres   Now tell me, Peggy, do you know what love is?

Peggy   Love, it is to give one fine things.

Wiseacres   How know you that, Peggy?

Peggy   Because, forsooth, Nuncle-Husband, Naunt said you lov'd me, and therefore that you gave me this Petticoat and Manto, and these Ribbonds, and this, and this . . .

Wiseacres   Indeed, indeed.

Doodle   Oh, she'll learn well in time . . .

Wiseacres   But now you are my wife, Peggy, and the love of a wife to her husband is to do all things that he desires and commands.

Peggy   Yes, forsooth.

Dashwell But, beside the love of a wife, Peggy, there is the duty of a wife, do you know what the duty of a wife is?

Peggy Duty, Nuncle, what's that?

Wiseacres I have not time to instruct you now in the whole duty of a wife, because business calls me away . . . I will therefore only inform you at present part of the duty.

Peggy Yes forsooth.

Enter **Arabella**, *looking from a balcony.*

Arabella I have heard all so far, but now I'll venture to peep, and see a little.

Enter **Aunt** *with cap-and-feather, a halberd and nightcap.*

Wiseacres That duty, Peggy, is to be done in this manner; here, put this on so . . . and now take this halberd in your hand . . . so. Now you shall be thus amply attired a great part of the night, for to watch while your husband is asleep is the duty of a wife here in London.

Peggy Yes forsooth, Nuncle. Oh dear Aunt, are not these very pretty things?

Arabella The fool's pleased. Oh, simplicity.

Wiseacres And though I shall not be present tonight,upon my pillow will I leave my nightcap, which is the emblem of me, your husband; and you must show all duty and reverence to that nightcap as if it were myself. So make your low curtsie to my nightcap.

Peggy Yes forsooth.

Arabella Oh, ridiculous.

Doodle Was there ever such a piece of simplicity as this?

Wiseacres Aunt, I commit Peggy to thy care; keep you the key of her chamber. About break of day go in and put her to bed. Let her sleep 'til noon. Then put her to bed in the afternoon again, and let her sleep 'til evening. Keep my doors shut all day and let her remain thus in ignorance. So now;

help to unharness her. There's my best Peggy. I wonder what kind of caution you give your wife; and what security you'll have of her in your absence.

Enter **Arabella**.

Arabella   A little better I hope than you have of your Mistress Ninny there.

Doodle   Wife!

Wiseacres   Is she here?

Arabella   I'll give her a lesson shall make her wiser.

Wiseacres   Go, withdraw . . .

Arabella   No, pray stay a little. These are not manners fit for city folk to show one so countrified.

Doodle   But, wife, we have business.

Arabella   But, husband; so do I. Look at me, husband.

Doodle   What frolic now, wife?

Arabella   You are going out of town, husband?

Doodle   Yes, wife.

Arabella   Do your duty then and come and kiss me.

Doodle   Oh. Ay, with all my heart, wife.

Arabella   Nay, nay; come not round, but over the bench. Nay, jump. Husband. Jump.

Doodle *jumps over.*

Doodle   So, there, wife.

Arabella   So, now back again this way; for the kiss you have earned, and another.

She goes round the bench and he jumps back again.

Doodle   Thou art such a wag, wife. So.

Arabella   Now there's a husband for you. Look you, little gentlewoman, your husband has taught you your duty, now do you teach him his, and make him do this every night and morning. You must teach your husband to come over and over, again and again, and make him glad to jump at it. I'll tell you another . . .

Wiseacres   Good neighbour, take your wife indoors!

Arabella   You teach your wife to reverence your nightcap. Look ye, Mistress Peggy; take his greasy nightcap thus and throw it downstairs, and him after it!

Wiseacres   Away, Peggy, away. This is a madwoman. See how she flings about; away or she will tear ye to pieces.

Peggy   Oh la! Aunt! Aunt!

Aunt   Ay, come away, Peggy, away . . .

Wiseacres   So, so. Lock her up in a room 'til we are gone.

Exeunt **Aunt** *and* **Peggy**.

Doodle   So, so enough, wife; thou hast had thy frolic.

Arabella   You are a fine man indeed; marry a woman to make a fool of her? You shall learn her more wit, or every wife in the parish shall be her schoolmistress.

Wiseacres   Well, your husband here may do what he please with you; let me alone to give my wife what instructions I see fit. I'll fain see what course he'll take with you now.

Doodle   Why, I will admit my wife has a forward wit . . . but needs little admonition.

Wiseacres   Pah.

Doodle   As you please; you shall hear now what I shall say to my wife. Well, dear . . . I would let you know that I am going and shall take my leave of you.

Arabella   Thank you, husband.

Doodle   Now, wife, I need give thee no instructions how to behave yourself while I am gone; I trust all to thy own discretion.

Arabella   I warrant you, husband; I have wit enough not to do myself any harm.

Doodle   Hear you this . . .

Arabella   And for any I do you, I have wit enough not to let you know it.

Doodle   My wife will have her jest, you see.

Wiseacres   And this, brother, you call her waggery.

Doodle   Ay, ay.

Arabella   Husband, business calls you from me, but you shall carry the key of your treasure with you. Though I bid you to make haste back again since every man has a key that will fit the same lock.

Doodle   Wife, I durst trust thee among all the picklocks in England . . . but I have only one thing to request of thee.

Arabella   What is that?

Doodle   Only this; that till my return, to all impertinent men, that ask you any questions, answer 'em with No. Let 'em say what they please, let your answer still be No.

Arabella   Husband, 'til I see you again I shall be sure to sing no other tune. All that I answer to any manner of man will be no and nothing but no, no no.

Doodle   You promise me?

Arabella   Yes. Sincerely.

Doodle   What will you forfeit if you break your word?

Arabella   The locket of diamonds you promised to buy me.

Doodle   Good. Bear witness, Mr Alderman. I have done, wife.

Wiseacres   And this is all the surety you take?

Arabella   A wiser course than you have taken I hope, that leaves your wife to walk about your chamber all night in armour, like an enchanted knight upon a fairyground.

Wiseacres We must make haste or we'll miss the tide.

Doodle Then, wife, adieu.

Arabella Ta ta, husband.

Exeunt **Wiseacres** *and* **Doodle**. *Enter* **Ramble** *and* **Townley** *over the wall.*

Arabella So, no is the word. We shall see what can be made of this no. But hold, what's this strange entrance?

Ramble As we counted them in, so they have gone out, Frank. Give me your hand.

Townley The inn step is kinder to a man's breeches, Ned.

Arabella 'Tis my mistaken lover, and the man I did mistake him for! I'll observe, and unobserved.

Arabella *hides.*

Townley Why do you pursue a face but glimpsed in the street when in your pocket you hold a sure note of promise?

Ramble 'Tis true the fair Eugenia awaits my coming to port, but this little Peggy veers me off course. E'en with a bird fast in the hand, methinks it foolish to pass by another's bush.

Townley Shall we not make our way to the inn; this chase is more suited to country half-wits. Did you not swear your own misfortune and my counsel had converted thee?

Ramble Indeed, and I shall never more make love my business, beyond this evening. You must wait here, concealed, and watch for their return. I shall make my entrance in the Italian style . . . and thus . . .

He climbs an ivy but is deposited back on the ground.

Upon reflection, Frank, I concur the fair Eugenia offers an easier entrance, the joys of which I shall forthwith avail myself.

Exit **Ramble**.

Townley   No good can come of this. This is no task for a
sober gentleman. I shall conceal myself, but would have this
venture fast concluded.

Townley *discovers* **Arabella**.

Townley   Madam. Forgive your most humble servant.

Arabella   No.

Townley   God's truth but I am, and would have you do so.

Arabella   No.

Townley   Madam, my trespass was not intended. I shall
take my leave.

Arabella   No.

Townley   You give me leave to stand and talk with you a
little?

Arabella   No.

Townley   Then, Lady Contrary, farewell.

Arabella   No.

Townley   There is no question but this is a Wife. Madam, is
your husband at home?

Arabella   No.

Townley   Then, madam, would you be hard-hearted if
there was a man that desired you?

Arabella   No.

Townley   By Jove, I would kiss thee for that, but that I fear
'twould put you out of humour.

Arabella   No.

Townley   That was kindly said. Would you refuse to accept
this ring from me?

Arabella   No.

Townley   And shall I wait on you to your door?

Arabella   No.

Townley   Ah, that spoils it again. Let us steal in unseen, my pretty little rogue.

Arabella   No.

Townley   Must I then be gone and leave you?

Arabella   No.

Townley   No, no, and ever no. Now, Lady, answer me at your peril: are you a maid?

Arabella   Ha, ha, ha!

Townley   Would you refuse a bed-fellow in his room tonight if you like the man?

Arabella   No.

Townley   If I took your hand, would you demur?

Arabella   No.

Townley   If I embraced you, would you thrust me away?

Arabella   No.

Townley   Or if I kissed thee, turn thy head?

Arabella   No.

Townley   Madam, is there any such liberty you would deny me?

Arabella   No.

Townley   And any time better than this present hour for us to so consort.

Arabella   No. No. No, no, no.

Exit **Arabella** *to the summer house, laughing.*

Townley   Here's a fair opportunity for an afternoon's diversion.

Exit **Townley**.

Scene Two

Eugenia's room in **Dashwell***'s house.*

Enter **Eugenia** *and* **Jane**.

Eugenia   Jane, did you deliver my letter to Mr Ramble?

Jane   Yes, madam, last night; I caught him in the street.

Eugenia   I wonder at his absence. Jane; be you at the door below and watch for his coming.

Jane   Yes, madam.

Exit **Jane**, *enter* **Loveday**.

Loveday   Madam, good evening to you.

Eugenia   What mean you, sir, to come hither uninvited?

Loveday   Nothing, madam, that one so virtuous might not assume. All day I have watched your husband's going out to get an opportunity to speak with you in private. Nay, blush not, madam, at anything that passed last night; what knowledge I have gathered of your secrets lies buried in this breast. The frolic I played last night was harmless, and I would not have proceeded so far, but to clear the house of a rival.

Eugenia   What mean you, sir?

Loveday   I mean an intruder to your affections, one that invades my right.

Eugenia   I understand you not, sir.

Loveday   Marriage has entitled you your husband's, your duty and obedience are his, but if you have any love to spare besides, I claim it as my due.

Eugenia   I confess you know my secrets, therefore may think to make me comply . . .

Loveday   No, lady; I scorn that.

Eugenia   And keep me in thrall by threatening to discover last night's transactions to my husband! That is a poor design.

Loveday   I have better intentions and a nobler claim. Look well on me; though in disguise, do you not know me?

Eugenia   Know you?

He offers his moustache, which she supposes an insect.

Loveday   Am I not like the one that loved you, and to whom you so often kindly said you could never love any other man? Is Loveday so lost in your remembrance? Have seven years so altered me?

Eugenia   Loveday? Is it you? Forgive my excess of wonder; your growth and the smallpox have so altered you. I scarce know you in anything but your voice, and even that is altered too.

His accent changes.

Loveday   You see, Eugenia, how subject we are to change. But my heart is still the same, and I wish yours were so too.

Eugenia   Be assured, Loveday, I can never hate the man I once lov'd so much.

Loveday   How young and innocent we were in our first loves; and all our vows sincere. But time and absence has effaced them quite, and your heart has taken new impressions. Oh, Eugenia, 'tis death to me to see you, and not to see you mine.

Eugenia   Speak not too much, my Loveday, lest you again raise the flame which was never quite extinct, for still it lies hot and glowing at my heart. But tell me; why came you in this disguise?

Loveday   When I returned from travel I heard the fatal news of your marriage, but excused you, because your friends deceived you.

Eugenia   Alas, they told me you were dead!

Loveday   That was our parents' plot to divide our affections. They writ the same to me of you.

Eugenia   Had I known you were living . . .

Loveday   Eugenia, say no more of that. Though you are married I claim a share in your affections. I cannot live without your kindness, and since you incline towards a gallant; I claim that title.

Eugenia   I confess I once loved you. Nor have my affections ever abated; the sight of you revives them again. Be you discreet, and I cannot be unkind.

Loveday   Blessed Eugenia!

Eugenia   My dear Loveday. How shall I recompense thy constancy?

Loveday   Love is the best reward of love. The hour is now inviting; your husband abroad, nobody to observe or restrain our desires . . . Say; shall we now? Blush not, nor turn thy head into my bosom, but to thy bed, my dear.

Eugenia   You have prevailed, and I have power to refuse you nothing. Wait. Jane! Stand there awhile and keep you silent. I must give some necessary orders to my maid.

Enter **Jane**.

Jane   Madam, I have spied Mr Ramble in the garden. By his many gestures he would gain admittance.

Eugenia   No matter for his coming now; my mind is altered.

Jane   Will you not see him then?

Eugenia   Not now. I will tell you my reasons another time.

Jane   As you wish, madam. I shall leave him to his pantomime.

Eugenia   Where are you going?

Jane   To make your bed.

Eugenia   No, no. Stay. I'll go to bed again for an hour.

Jane   I'll lay it smooth then for you.

Eugenia   Hold. Don't come in, go down, and remain below until I call you. Dismiss Mr Ramble and watch my husband's coming.

Jane   Yes, madam.

Exit **Jane**. **Loveday** *unbuttoned*.

Eugenia   Come, dearest, we must make . . . haste.

Loveday   Come to my arms, dear kind creature, and let me gaze upon thy charms, before the curtains are drawn round us, and day is shut from our sight. Thus I could look, and kiss, and hug, for ever. Oh, I am in an ecstasy of joy.

Eugenia   Came you hither to talk, my dear?

Loveday   Oh dear soul, such benevolent a reprimand. Come, now to bed. To bed, that we may plunge in bliss, and dive in the sweet ocean of delight.

Eugenia   Proceed where you will; I durst may follow.

A knock on the door.

Jane (*without*)   Madam, my master is below, and just coming up to you.

Eugenia   Oh, good wench, run down and stop him a little.

Jane   He's coming upstairs now.

Loveday   Where shall I hide myself?

Eugenia   Cover yourself in the bed.

She covers him in the bed, shuts the curtains, and sits upon a cushion by the bedside, as reading. Enter **Dashwell** *and* **Jane**.

Jane   Pray, sir, don't go in there, I am just going to make the bed.

Dashwell   Well, I shan't stay . . . what is your mistress doing?

Jane   What she is always doing, sir. Praying I think . . .

Dashwell   Oh, yonder she is . . . come wife, prethee lay by thy book. I did never see the like of thee, thou art always reading one good book or another.

Exit **Jane**.

Eugenia   I had just done, husband, and was coming down . . . that Jane might clean the room. Come, will you go below?

Dashwell   Stay a little, wife, I came only to tell thee I must go down-river. And to tell thee the news . . . the Bride and Bridegroom are come from church. What luck Mr Alderman will have in the marriage, I know not. Methinks the Bride is more fit to play with a doll than a husband. God's teeth, a Cock Sparrow would be too much for her.

Eugenia   How you talk, husband . . .

Dashwell   Wife . . . come hither, wife.

Eugenia   And who was there at the Wedding?

Dashwell   Only Alderman Doodle and myself, and an old woman the Bride calls Aunt. Come hither, wife.

Eugenia   Jane!

Eugenia   Prethee, husband, let us go down.

Dashwell   Prethee, wife, to bed!

Enter **Jane**.

Jane   Madam?

Dashwell   Jane, go down and prepare your mistress's . . . porridge.

Jane   Sir, 'tis nearly supper-time.

Dashwell   Eh? Then fetch me coffee, and my tobacco-box . . .

Jane   Lord, sir, you won't offer to take tobacco here, in my mistress's chamber?

Dashwell   Hark, somebody knocks.

Jane No, sir, no . . .

Dashwell Eh? Pouh, pish. Here, take the Key of my counting-house and fetch the packet of Letters that lies in the window.

Jane You know, sir, I could never open that scurvy door in my life.

Dashwell Go, say I.

Jane Yes, master.

Exit **Jane**.

Dashwell Now, wife . . . Pox on that dull wench . . . she has put me off. I shan't have such a mind again this month. Well, wife, I'll leave thee, I must catch the tide and see to business. Fare thee well, I'll come and see you before night.

Eugenia As you please, husband.

Exit **Dashwell**.

His absence never was more wish'd . . . are you not in a sweat, sir?

Loveday I am almost smother'd. If he had proceeded in his kindness to you, I should have had a fine time on't.

Eugenia Jane's coming was very lucky.

Loveday Would he not have been put off?

Eugenia Yes, he's never very troublesome.

Loveday Eugenia, let us bed with all the eager haste that ever Lovers made.

Jane (*within*) Hold, sir, hold, you must not go in.

Ramble (*within*) You are mistaken, Mrs Jane.

Jane (*within*) My mistress charg'd me to the contrary.

Ramble (*within*) You brought me a letter from her, she sent for me . . .

Eugenia   Hark, I think I hear him coming upstairs again. Shut the Curtain.

Enter **Ramble** *followed by* **Jane**.

Eugenia   Who is it, Jane?

Ramble   'Tis I, your humble servant.

Jane   Madam, I did open my window to dismiss the gentleman and he would not have me close it again until he had secured his entrance.

Ramble   I received your letter, kiss'd it a thousand times, and made what haste I could to obey your summons.

Eugenia   Things are alter'd since, my husband . . .

Ramble   He's safe, madam, I saw him go out.

Eugenia   He's gone but across the street, I am sure he will not stay long, let me beg you therefore to shorten your visit.

Ramble   You seem to drive me hence. But yet you sent for me.

Eugenia   By that you see my kindness, were it convenient. I dare not run too great a hazard, it imports me, sir, to be wary. Wherefore if you love me, or ever hope for my kindness, go away now for fear of a mischief.

Ramble   We have not yet talk'd half enough . . . you have given me no account of the mischief you made last night. You should know that other gentleman is my intimate friend and acquaintance.

Eugenia   I am apt to believe you thought more than was, and that he spoke more than he ought. We have not the time to come to a complete understanding, therefore I beg you would leave me at present.

Ramble   I dare refuse you nothing, but methinks so fair an opportunity should not be lost, your husband gone abroad, you undress'd, your bed there, I here . . .

Dashwell (*without*)   Jane, Jane, where are you?

Eugenia   Undone, that's my husband's voice, coming
upstairs.

Ramble   I'll under the bed . . .

Eugenia   You can't, it's too low.

Ramble   I'll into't then.

Eugenia   Hold, no. No, my husband's come home to bed,
he's not well.

Ramble   What shall I do?

Jane (*without*)   Have a care, sir, have a care . . .

Eugenia   Draw your Sword, be angry . . . threaten. Swear
you'll kill . . .

Ramble   Who, your husband?

Eugenia   Anybody . . . no matter . . . hunt about as if you
look'd for somebody.

Enter **Dashwell** *and* **Jane**.

Jane   I say have a care . . . have a care . . .

Dashwell   Have a care of what, you silly ninny. Wife, what
makes you tremble?

Eugenia   O Lord, husband, I am so frighted . . .

Dashwell   Hau! A drawn Sword . . . what's he there? Who
are you, sir? What would you have, sir?

Ramble   Have, sir . . .

Eugenia   Indeed, sir, he is not here. Pray be pacified . . .

Ramble   I'll be the death of him; his blood shall pay for the
affront.

Dashwell   Know I not thy face, sir?

Eugenia   Indeed, sir, he is not here.

Ramble   Come, come, down on your knees all of you and
confess.

Dashwell   What means this, wife?

Ramble   Down on your knees, sir.

Dashwell   Knees, sir?

Eugenia   He is not here upon my word, sir . . .

Dashwell   He is not here indeed, sir . . . Who is't, wife?

Ramble   He must be here, I follow'd him.

Jane   Indeed, sir, he went out again.

Ramble   No, he must be hereabouts, I'll not leave a corner unsearch'd . . . Hau . . .

He counterfeits a rage, throws open the curtains, pulls off the bedclothes and discovers **Loveday** *in the bed.*

Loveday   Hu!

Ramble   Ha!

Eugenia   Ah! I swoon!

Dashwell   A man in my bed.

Eugenia *screeks . . . runs to* **Ramble***, catches him on his arm and swounds.*

Jane   Oh hold, sir, for Heaven's sake, my mistress swounds. She'll die away.

Ramble   Madam, be not frighted, I'll not meddle with him now for your sake.

Dashwell   What means all this?

Ramble   Your house shall at present be his Sanctuary, and protect the man that hath done me such injuries, but when I meet him abroad, let him guard well his throat, had he twenty lives he should not live one hour after.

Dashwell   Pray, sir, let me know the meaning of this, and how the young man has offended you.

Ramble   I cannot think on't without rage, let them tell you.

Dashwell   What have you done to the Gentleman to provoke him?

Loveday   Done to him, sir . . . no great matter . . . but that . . . a . . .

Eugenia   I'll tell you, husband . . . Jane being in the street and seeing this Gentleman pass by, was so foolish to shriek and cry out, the Devil! The Gentleman pressing to know her meaning, she told him she saw the Devil in his shape last night; and how one in this house rais'd him in his likeness; upon this the Gentleman being incens'd rush'd into the house to look for the young man, who, hearing him threaten, slip'd away and ran in here for shelter; and had not Jane and I hid him in my bed he had certainly been murther'd.

Dashwell   You silly baggage.

Jane   Truly, sir, it was my fright, the Devil last night and this Gentleman were so alike . . .

Dashwell   Nay he was very like him, that's the truth on't.

Ramble   Sir, now you know the reason, I hope you'll excuse my intruding into your house, and I beg your pardon, madam, for frighting you . . . as for that Conjuror, let him beware how he stirs over your threshold. Your servant, your servant . . . Oh, false, damn'd false woman!

Exit **Ramble**.

Dashwell   Jane, go down and lock the door after him.

Exit **Jane**.

Eugenia   How happen'd it that you return'd so luckily, husband?

Dashwell   By especial providence I think, the Master of the Ship having come to us on his initiative. And I am glad it fell out so, since my coming sav'd a man's life, for ought I know.

Eugenia   Indeed so am I, husband.

Loveday   And I.

Dashwell   And you, sir. I have received news for you. My correspondent in Bristol, to whom I recommended you, has sent word he is happy to employ and entertain you, and has promptly provided for your journey. You are to travel tomorrow and he says you must go very early.

Loveday   I thank you, sir, for your patronage.

Dashwell   Well then, all's done. I have writ a short note for you to travel with, and will fetch it.

Exit **Dashwell**.

Loveday   Oh, unlucky accident. He has cut off all my hopes. I cannot think of parting from you.

Eugenia   But you must go from hence.

Loveday   Not to gain one hour's privacy, one minute's enjoyment of my love. Both to be resolved and willing, and yet to be disappointed. Dear Eugenia; I am almost mad.

Eugenia   Despair not, Loveday, for now I shall try my art in spite of fortune. The cards are now in my hand, and I'll deal once more in hopes of better luck.

Loveday   Kind, dear woman, but how?

Eugenia   I hear him. Hide you there, but make no noise.

Exit **Loveday**, *enter* **Dashwell**.

Dashwell   Where is our visitor?

Eugenia   Husband, I sent him to his room.

Dashwell   How so? I must give him my letter so he may be gone early in the morning.

Eugenia   But I think it not appropriate you should recommend him to any friend, or entertain him further yourself. He is not the person you take him for.

Dashwell   What mean you?

Eugenia   I mean he is an impudent rascal, and only fit to be kicked out of doors.

Dashwell   What has he done?

Eugenia   I know not whether he made a false construction of my extra-ordinary care to hide him in my bed, but he had the impudence e'en now when you were gone to tell me that his coming here was for my sake, and that it would break his heart to leave the house 'til he had accomplished his design.

Dashwell   A rogue. So much I had begun to suspect!

Eugenia   And said he hoped, since time allowed him not further opportunities of courtship, I would without ceremony consent to steal out of bed from you when you were fast asleep, and slipping on my nightgown, meet him in the summer house.

Dashwell   The dainty rogue.

Eugenia   To be revenged of him for his insolence; I would have you dress yourself in a nightgown and cap, and go down in the dark, take a good cudgel in your hand and drub him soundly, then turn him out of doors. You may let Jane be with you to help you.

Dashwell   That shall be his punishment! I would not for a hundred pounds I had sent him where I intended, the insolent dog. Lose his labour? I'll give him the fruits of his labour.

Eugenia   Here is a nightgown.

Dashwell   Let me put it on quickly.

Eugenia   No, no. Go downstairs and dress you there, and hide yourself in the summer house 'til he comes.

Dashwell   I'll baulk him for making assignations! The rogue, the dog. The son of a cur. . .

Exit **Dashwell**.

Eugenia   Come, sir, come from your post.

Loveday   Dear creature; thou witty rogue.

Eugenia   An hour is our own by this invention.

Loveday   Let us retire, Eugenia, and make the best use on't we can.

Eugenia   But how shall it end?

Loveday   I can think of nothing but thee at present, and the Heaven I am going to enjoy. Now we shall fly to it and plunge into bliss and be nought but rapture, all ecstasy. Already I am all on fire, my soul is in a blaze. And whilst we talk I burn in vain.

Eugenia   All talk is vain when opportunity requires performance!

Scene Three

A bedchamber in **Wiseacres***' house.*

Enter **Ramble**, *dishevelled, as from the balcony.*

Ramble   This may be beyond the remit of a gentleman, but my daring is born of a noble and virtuous desperation. Someone comes. To be sure 'tis too heavy a step for a lady, nor a husband either.

Peggy *enters in armour and walks by the bedside.*

Ramble   What monster is this haunts a pleasant household?

Peggy *has difficulty with her duties, and removes her helmet.*

Ramble   Pretty creature . . . do not start.

Peggy   You are that same gentleman.

Ramble   What art thou doing at this time of night?

Peggy   I am a wife an't please you, this is the duty of a wife here in London.

Ramble   Oh, simplicity.

Peggy   Are you here, sir, to visit my husband?

Ramble   No, indeed to visit thee.

Peggy   I did so believe you to be a kind gentleman.

Ramble   How long have you been married, pretty miss?

Peggy   I was married this morning betimes.

Ramble   And who dressed you thus prettily?

Peggy   My Uncle-Husband.

Ramble   Your Uncle-Husband?

Peggy   Yes, my Uncle-Husband.

Ramble   And to what end did he dress you thus?

Peggy   Indeed, that I might watch whilst my husband sleeps.

Ramble   Sweet thing, you have been sorely imposed upon.

Peggy   'Tis but my duty.

Ramble   And is this all you know of the Duty of a Wife?

Peggy   This is as far as I have learned yet, but Uncle will teach me more when he comes back.

Ramble   Pretty Peggy, would you not thank a man that would teach you your lesson perfect before he comes?

Peggy   Oh, yes!

Ramble   Then first, Mrs Peggy, you must lay by this halberd, and these things, and come to your bed.

Ramble *sets about opening the armour.*

Peggy   Indeed; what is to be learned there?

Ramble   The most significant schooling.

Peggy   Oh, sir.

Ramble *drops armour on his foot.*

Peggy   Oh, sir, are you injured?

Ramble   'Tis of no consequence.

Peggy   But can you walk, sir.

Ramble   Indeed I can, Miss Peggy, but I have no plans to do so, for I shall stay with you tonight and take pains to instruct you in the entire duty of a wife.

Peggy   Will you indeed? But sir, they told me last night that such a one as you would eat me.

Ramble   Nay, Peggy, but we must pay special tutelage to thine own appetite.

Peggy   But my Uncle-Husband said I was to wear these things and not go to bed 'til morning that Aunt came to me, and that I was to do so all night, and he will be angry, and Aunt told me God won't bless me if I anger my husband.

Ramble *takes fire tongs to the armour.*

Ramble   But your Uncle-Husband came to me and told me he was mistaken, and your Aunt most heartily agreed and bid me come to you and teach you the right duty and which I was at prayers this morning I could swear God himself bid me tell you that you must go to bed and do as I'd have you do.

Peggy   Oh then indeed, I'll to bed and you shall teach me.

Ramble   Ay! Ay! Do dear pretty Peggy, and make haste. Never was there such a little fool as this. Now, my little sweet dear piece of innocence, thou little simple pretty foolish thing. What first lesson shall it pleasure us to undertake? I am almost out of my senses with joy.

A cry of 'fire' off.

Peggy   Hark, sir; the house is on fire.

Ramble   No. No indeed, it is not.

Peggy   Did you not hear 'em cry 'fire' in the street just now?

Ramble   Yes, but they cry a great many things here in London, as 'Hot 'Taters' and such.

Peggy   I have heard them, 'tis so, and 'Oranges and Lemons' too.

Ramble   Ay, Oranges and Lemons also.

Peggy   Then, sir, the fire must be for sale and you may commence thy teaching.

Enter **Aunt**, *with a pan on fire, with* **Scullery Boy**.

Scullery Boy   Fire!

Aunt   Fire!

Scullery Boy   Fire!

Aunt   Fire!

Ramble   Fire!

Peggy   Deeds, Aunt; have you bought some?

Aunt   This pan has took blaze and catched hold of the kitchen chimney . . .

Peggy   Oh, naughty fire.

Ramble   Old dame, be still!

Aunt   The Devil! The Devil has been upon thee!

Ramble   Do you decline to have the fiend extinguish thee?

Aunt   This is a righteous fire; no Devil's. Out, sir; out! I shall singe thy tail.

Ramble   Madam, I . . . farewell.

Aunt   Foolish child. Low wretched man.

Exit **Ramble** *pursued by* **Aunt** *and* **Scullery Boy**.

Peggy   To be sure London is a quite livelier place than the country. Though I would not have been so disappointed in my education.

Enter **Townley**, *unbraced, as from the balcony*.

Townley   I heard a cry of fire.

Peggy   Yet another visitor!

Townley   And thought to rescue my good friend and thee.

Peggy   Sir, there is no fire worth your fears, and your friend has departed, hurriedly.

Townley   Then, madam; you are safe.

Peggy   But disappointed, sir. Your friend was about to instruct me in my married duties for the benefit of my husband.

Townley   Indeed. A noble enterprise.

Peggy   Now he has rushed off and I shall learn nothing 'til another day.

Townley   Sweet Lady, to be in despond does not become thee. There are perhaps other tutors.

Peggy   But, sir, are you familiar with the subject?

Townley   I have been of recent study, madam. And I have a growing reputation.

Peggy   And might I be your special pupil, sir?

Townley   Hey ho. I'll forswear another bottle. (*Aside.*) Is it not a fine thing to grant horns to the cuckold and cuckolder both! – I'll mouse thee and touse thee and tumble thee 'til morn.

Act Five

Scene One

Communal gardens behind **Wiseacres'**, **Doodle**'s *and* **Dashwell**'s *houses.*

Enter **Ramble** *on fire, pursued by* **Aunt** *and* **Scullery Boy**.

Aunt (*off*)   Vile seducer! Lewd villain!

Ramble   Not to be outwitted by old women and potboys, I have doubled back to where they will not have the wit to look.

Scullery Boy (*off*)   He came back this way with thought to outwit us.

Ramble   Oh, rats to 'em.

Ramble *hides.*

Aunt   I'll beat his wits from his skull ere he escapes me.

Scullery Boy   This way, missus. All vermin run for cover.

Aunt   I'll cut off his tail and more besides.

Exit **Aunt** *and* **Scullery Boy**. *Enter* **Doodle** *and* **Wiseacres**. **Ramble** *hides up a tree.*

Doodle   It was very well the master of the ship came up as he did and saved us from a fool's errand. It would have vexed you to have lost the first night's lodging with your Bride for a cold voyage of no purpose.

Wiseacres   Indeed. Now will I go to my little wife, whom I shall find upon duty, taking short turns around my bedside. Aunt!

Wiseacres *knocks.*

Doodle   I think it a great deal of cruelty in you so to torment a poor innocent. I will go home to my wife and set her tongue at liberty.

Aunt (*within*) Who's there?

Wiseacres 'Tis I.

Enter **Aunt**.

Aunt Oh, indeed. I did not expect you back tonight.

Wiseacres What smell is this about the door?

Doodle Here's a smell of soot and burning.

Aunt Alas, after you went a pot caught the kitchen chimney on fire. I was frighted out of my wits.

Wiseacres How, fire?

Aunt Thank providence it was quickly out. It did no great harm, but to interupt Peggy as she . . . went to bed.

Wiseacres Peggy? To bed?

Aunt Indeed, sir.

Wiseacres Contrary to my orders, going to bed?

Aunt But without my knowledge, sir.

Wiseacres Into bed in contempt of my commands! Monstrous!

Doodle Now where's your caution?

Aunt Nay, I told her you would be very angry.

Wiseacres And what said she to that?

Aunt She said no, you would not be angry.

Wiseacres Bid her slip on her nightgown and come down to me to acknowledge her fault! I'll turn you out of doors for this, and for such another I'll send her out after you. Go call her down to me!

Aunt Yes an't please ye, sir.

Wiseacres Leave your ducking and dropping and tell her quickly.

Exit **Aunt**.

Aunt (*off*)   Peggy! Mistress Peggy!

Doodle   Nay, nay, Mr Alderman; hear the business before you are so angry.

Wiseacres   You must know I think severely on this; for a wife who would not obey the temperate and agreeable instructions of a devoted and concerned husband may not be trusted either in those things of greater consequence.

Enter **Townley** *above, hurriedly.*

Doodle   Whilst I would never trust a simple wife, I am indisposed to believe even the simplest could have erred so already.

Townley *leaps to the ground and discovers* **Doodle** *and* **Wiseacres**.

Doodle   Ha!

Wiseacres   God's teeth!

Ramble (*aside*)   For one so fond of an inn, I observe my friend Frank Townley does greatly frequent ladies' chambers.

Wiseacres   And who are you, sir?

Townley   Um . . . Where is the fire, sir?

Wiseacres   The fire?

Townley   And what knave has stole away my ladder?

Wiseacres   What mean you, sir?

Townley   To put out the fire I saw when I heard the cry of fire and climbed the wall to bring aid to any endangered by the fire that . . . was on fire.

Doodle   Good citizen, I thought the fire was done before we came.

Townley   Ay, sir, some time, but I have had experience in the fortitude and insistence of that element and would take all pains to be sure it was out before I went on my way.

Wiseacres   This sounds a considerate citizen.

Doodle   I smell other than cinders and soot. What think you now sir, of your simple wife?

Wiseacres   You may think as you please of this man's jumping from the balcony, and make false conjectures, but you are mistaken. I am assured by this gentleman's honest demeanour he did but commit an act of great courage.

Ramble (*aside*)   And will needs find greater courage ere I confront him.

Doodle   Nay, if this man's tumbling out of your wife's chamber window is no argument, I find you are wilfully resolved to maintain your error or have lost thy wits.

Wiseacres   By your leave, I am not yet convinced I was in the wrong.

Doodle   Good night, sir. Wife! Whoever is awake; come down and open the door! 'Tis not your wife who is a fool, sir, but you yourself.

Wiseacres   Say you so, sir? Doubt you the word of this good gentleman! He did come to my house to put out a fire!

Doodle   Methinks to light one, more likely, by putting a taper to your wife.

Townley   Sir, I do object to your lewd conjecture. Indeed, sir, I was otherwise engaged before the cry of fire and thus could not have approached this Gentleman's wife so rudely.

Wiseacres   Hear you this? Expand upon your explanation, sir!

Townley   Now I think on it, 'twas such an unusual adventure to tell it you would convince you both most surely, for nothing so unlikely could be thought of in aid of an excuse.

Doodle   Pray what was it, sir?

Townley   Well, if we be gentlemen . . . earlier tonight it was my good fortune to offer my service to a lady. One other than your wife, sir, be assured. I began to make some little courtships to her, but to everything I said she answered nothing but No.

Wiseacres   No, sir?

Townley   Yes, sir. Not a word could I get from her but no, no, no.

Wiseacres   Nothing but no?

Townley   Whatever I asked her was no.

Doodle   Hum . . . So, sir . . .

Wiseacres   Pray, sir, continue.

Townley   I asked her if I should be her servant; she said no.

Doodle   Such a response would be to the honour of a lady.

Enter **Arabella** *above.*

Townley   Indeed, sir, but then, perceiving she had taken up an odd humour to say nothing but no and had resolved to give no other answer, I studied to ask such questions, that if she answered no, it would please me well.

Wiseacres   Very good, sir. Hear you this, Mr Alderman?

Exit **Arabella**.

Doodle   What of it?

Wiseacres   Well, sir, and how then?

Townley   I asked her then if she would not be angry if I went indoors with her, and she said no.

Wiseacres   No, Brother!

Townley   If she would refuse me as a bed-fellow; no.

Wiseacres   No, she said again.

Townley   If that I embraced her, would she thrust me away? She said; no.

Wiseacres   No.

Townley   If there was any such liberty she would deny me?
No!

Wiseacres   No. No. She said no, Brother!

Doodle   No, well . . . I observe that . . . humph.

Ramble (*aside*)   What stars conspire round Frank Townley's
head that he does make such easy acquaintance with these
women?

Townley   So now I tell you, Gentlemen, I led her to this
very summer house . . .

Enter **Engine** *with wine.*

Engine   Sir, my mistress sent me out with this wine that you
might take a nightcap.

Doodle   It is late, certainly. Let us go inside.

Wiseacres   Pray listen, sir; let him go on.

Townley   In ran she, in ran I. Onto the bench she throws
herself, onto the bench throw I myself by her . . .

Engine   Pray drink, sir . . .

Townley   Or upon her as you may guess.

Engine   'Tis a special vintage.

Wiseacres   And not a word but no said the lady all this
while. No was the word, Brother.

Doodle   Ay, yes, yes. So I hear.

Engine   Drink, sir! Drink to that kind lady's good health,
and that it may continue.

Townley   To the health of the Negative Lady. Long life
indeed.

Doodle   Long life.

Ramble (*aside*)   And a short one to you, Frank Townley, and
the gout along with it.

Townley *drinks and discovers his ring in the glass.*

Townley   Ha. A ring in my mouth, and my ring.

Enter **Arabella**.

Arabella   Gentlemen, husband. It grows late; will you gossip all night? Am I of your acquaintance, sir?

Wiseacres   Well, sir?

Doodle   Well, sir?

Townley   . . .

Arabella   I had overheard your story from the window.

Wiseacres   Come sir; let us have the rest of your story.

Ramble (*aside*)   Indeed I would hear it too.

Townley   Well . . . To make my story short . . . As I prepared to . . .

Wiseacres   To tumble this jade . . .

Townley   To share affections with this innocent creature I had thus outwitted . . . for 'tis certain she should be pitied for my cruel usage . . .

Wiseacres   Hang it all, sir; continue.

Townley   . . . I did fall off the bench and strike my head against a large stone. And with such a fall I waked out of my dream.

Wiseacres   Wha?

Doodle   Why then, this is all but a dream?

Townley   Yes, sir.

Wiseacres   How! A dream?

Townley   Ay, sir; a dream.

Wiseacres   You have not said it was a dream.

Townley   Could such a strange encounter be other than

such? To be sure, it could not happen with credence e'en in the Playhouse.

Ramble (*aside*)   It is a wonder to observe such wit from one so ordinarily witless.

Doodle   This is wonderful. A dream it was, for certain.

Arabella   But is it not strange, husband, that this gentleman should dream a Lady who would behave so alike as to how you instructed me?

Wiseacres   I would warrant that's odd, would you not, Alderman?

Arabella   Truly, sir, I wondered all the while where the story would end. It was so pat to our intrigue.

Doodle   Truly, wife, I knew not what to think on't, 'til I heard it was but a dream.

Arabella   Well, sir, I must beg your pardon if I have made you a cuckold . . .

Doodle   How, madam?

Arabella   But 'twas in a dream, sir.

Townley   So sweet a dream I could wish to dream it a thousand times o'er.

Arabella   I can almost fancy but that I am in a dream still.

Townley   Methinks this feels more like a dream than the other.

*Enter **Aunt** and **Peggy**.*

Aunt   She is here an't please you.

Townley   I'll bid you all good night.

Wiseacres   No sir, stand by. I would speak to you further concerning this unlikely dream. Wait while I must chastise my wife, then we shall take a drink together. Peggy; come hither.

Peggy   Welcome home, Nuncle-Husband.

Wiseacres   Peggy, how durst you neglect your duty to me your husband and go to bed?

Peggy   But I did not neglect my duty.

Wiseacres   Why, went you not to bed? Hau?

Peggy   Yes, but I went to bed to learn my duty.

Wiseacres   Did I not teach you what you were to do?

Peggy   But he taught me a better duty than that you showed me; a great deal.

Wiseacres   He? What he?

Doodle   What he is this?

Peggy   He that came before the fire and asked me why I walked so and when I told him he said that was but the first duty and he would show me all the rest of the nightly duties of a wife, and that you had sent him so to do.

Wiseacres   The Devil he did. Stand, sir!

Wiseacres *draws upon* **Townley**.

Tempt me not. I shall run you through.

Ramble (*aside*)   Now might my friend be judged harshly, wrongly, and justly and all at once!

Townley   Have a care with your weapon, sir, for a gentleman such as I does easily bleed.

Peggy   Nuncle, husband, do not threaten so.

Wiseacres   Continue, Peggy; what next occurred.

Peggy   Why nothing, for there was a cry of fire, and the man rushed away.

Aunt   Indeed it is true, sir; discovering the rogue I did chase him off.

Wiseacres   And this is the man did promise you these . . . lessons?

Peggy   Why no, sir; it was not he.

Townley   You hear this, sir? The man did nothing and was not me neither.

Wiseacres   Be sure and tell me the truth, Peggy.

Peggy   No, sir, certainly. This is the man who came to save me from the fire.

Wiseacres   Ha! Hear you that, Alderman.

Doodle   Indeed.

Wiseacres   It is as he says; he came to give assistance.

Townley   Ever your servant, sir.

Peggy   This man made no promises, but gave great assistance, and taught the very things the other had promised.

Wiseacres   Wha!

Peggy   I could not think the other could have been a better teacher neither.

Ramble (*aside*)   Here's proof; my former friend has sprung another snare I was at pains to set!

Doodle   Pray, Peggy; what did he teach you?

Peggy   Nay I can't tell you, but I have learned a great deal and, Uncle, if I were in bed I could show you!

Wiseacres   You are a baggage!

Peggy   Indeed, Uncle, I had forgot you told me I must call you husband, but Uncle-Husband it was ten times a better duty than that you taught me.

Wiseacres   Very pleasant.

Peggy   Yes, yes. So pleasant I could do such duty all night long. Though after he taught me my lesson two or three times, I fell fast asleep.

Wiseacres   Hahhh!

Ramble (*aside*) Lay on, sir; do your worst. Another blow, surely, would be just.

Peggy But Nuncle, do not treat him so. When I share with you all I have learnt, I'm sure you will be best pleased.

Townley Peace, sir; the lady has confused herself. I have imparted to her no such knowledge, nor had any of her. This, would you but give me respite, could I prove to your satisfaction.

Wiseacres I shall hold, sir, but only that you might lie with your last breath and thus speed to hell upon it. And then send her swiftly after.

Aunt Oh, mercy.

Peggy Aunt, is it something I have done has made Nuncle-Husband angry?

Townley When I did enter the lady's room to search for fire, she was asleep.

Aunt 'Tis true. Have patience.

Wiseacres Were you sleeping?

Peggy Indeed, sir; when Aunt woke me to say you were come home, and the man was gone.

Townley As I stood close she did toss in her sleep and briefly open her eyes to me.

Wiseacres And it was this man you did see?

Peggy Indeed it was he but methought . . .

Wiseacres You did think?

Peggy Methought I know not what.

Wiseacres This may answer it. You only thought 'twas so. 'Twas all but your thought.

Doodle How's this?

Wiseacres Your glimpse of this man was midwife to a dream.

Doodle   Impossible.

Wiseacres   There was no teacher, nor no lessons.

Peggy   But there was though . . .

Wiseacres/Aunt/Townley   No there was not.

Peggy   But indeed . . . and indeed . . . Uncle-Husband, there was.

Wiseacres   Peace I tell you; there was not. 'Twas all but a dream.

Townley   A dream.

Doodle   A dream?

Arabella   Well, to be sure, Gentlemen, there has been so much dreaming I would swear this was more likely a dream that we do now walk in and talk in and make but little sense of.

Doodle   Hark you, Brother Alderman, what think you of a fool for a wife now?

Wiseacres   What think you of a witty one?

Townley   What's the meaning of all this, madam?

Arabella   They don't know themselves.

Ramble (*aside*)   My enforced seclusion does bring on the cramp. I would they'd all retire. I must adjust my purchase, thus.

Peggy   Methinks it was a very strange dream had quite so many strangers in't. For, Nuncle-Husband, there was surely another man . . .

Wiseacres   Be silent! There were no other men but that morpheous commanded.

Doodle   No other men and be done. Let us be agreed that he talks nonsense who would have it that all wives are faithless, that *are* not.

Wiseacres   Or that rakes and seducers fall from the very trees, that *do* not!

Ramble *falls from a tree into an ornamental pond.*

Ramble   Aaarhg!

Doodle   Ha!

Wiseacres   Servants, hither! What Devil are you, sir?!

Arabella   My unlucky lover.

Doodle   God's truth, it is the Devil indeed. I have seen him conjured once before! Come not close to me, thou fiend!

Servants *enter and take* **Ramble**.

Wiseacres   Hold him for a rogue! He is a fiend, you say?

Doodle   Ay, sir, and haunts your tree!

Wiseacres   Pish.

Doodle   Or can live in cupboards too.

Ramble   Good sirs, I am neither a rogue nor fiend nor any rough sort of man, but a gentleman who has found himself through no ill deeds . . . up a tree.

Wiseacres   Wretched cur! Explain thyself.

Townley   If you had been asleep and dreamt much, 'twould be beneficial to you.

Ramble   If you had been to Dover and enlisted thyself, 'twould be beneficial also.

Wiseacres   If your explanation be not fit, you shall be trounced as a hooligan or hanged as a thief! Speak, blackguard!

Peggy   Oh, Nuncle-Husband, do not hang him, for he stole nothing that I saw.

Townley   That's true, I'll warrant.

Peggy   This is the man who proves it was no dream at all!!

He did nothing but offer to teach me the duty of a wife; didn't you, sir?

Ramble   No. No.

Wiseacres   Go, wife; go. You are in a dream still.

Peggy   Oh but it was no dream though. This is the gentleman that offered theory and this is the gentleman in practice.

Doodle   Ha, ha, ha. There's simplicity for you.

Arabella   Well, Mr Alderman, is your foolish wife so very innocent?

Doodle   Methinks, sir, you are neither a spirit nor a figment, but one who hides in cupboards and up trees awaiting opportunity.

Townley   Indeed, and in cellar-holes too, disguised as an African.

Ramble   Mr Townley, you have kept better company than I tonight and I would so beg your silence!

Wiseacres   In cellar-holes? Then, Alderman Doodle, he has laid siege to your property also!

Doodle   Let's have done with further conjecture and turn him in for a common thief!

Wiseacres   Do so!

Ramble   Kind sirs, desist. Do not arrest me for I am neither thief, spirit, African, seducer, Devil nor dream.

Wiseacres   Then, sir, what are you?

Ramble   I am, sir . . . a catcher of rats. An employment which does oblige me to seek my quarry in the strangest quarters, such as cellar-holes, cupboards, and up trees . . .

Doodle   Up trees?

Ramble   Indeed, sir, the rat chased from one place will make ingenious use of another.

Townley   So much is evident.

Ramble   And in the course of my endeavours, gentlemen, have been spied by my lady thus and put into a dream, and by this honest gentleman and mistook for a thief, and in pursuit of half a dozen verminous creatures of no mean aspect, by you all this night for a man of no virtue. My profession is a mean one, but honourable, as I hope you now will find me. For to grant honour to one who deserves it is to claim honour for oneself, and for one's wife too, if ever it had been in doubt.

Wiseacres   I would believe you speak honestly, sir.

Doodle   Ay, and wisely too.

Peggy   But be there rats in trees?

Wiseacres   Shush.

Enter **Dashwell**, *in his wife's attire, and* **Jane**.

Dashwell   Hark you, Mr Alderman, and Mr Alderman there.

Townley   Heaven! What foul fiend is that?

Arabella   Neighbour Dashwell!

Doodle   Turned Coquette!

Wiseacres   What means this?

Dashwell   You'll see anon. But pray in the interim leave your disputes of a witty wife or a foolish wife, and learn by example presently that you are both in the wrong, as I told you before. And now be convinced what 'tis to have a zealous wife.

Wiseacres   Why I pray, what hast to say as to that matter?

Dashwell   A villain has tempted my wife to meet him in the summer house to commit his felonious purpose against my honour. She has proved herself a virtuous, good woman, and has acquainted me with the wicked machinations, and has advised me to entertain him here in the dark.

Ramble   Hark you, Frank Townley, is this an endeavour of yours or an intrigue of mine?

Townley   I know not.

Jane   Hark, sir; the garden door unlocks. The traitor is coming.

Dashwell   Hist! Then be silent all, I pray. Put out your candles and conceal yourselves. But do not help the rogue, though he cry out never so, for it will be I that do caress him.

Doodle   Brave sir; lay him on.

Wiseacres   Lay him on soundly.

All conceal themselves as **Loveday** *enters with a hunting whip.*

Dashwell   Jane, I hear him come. Stand close; be ready.

Jane   I warrant you, sir.

Loveday   Oh, sweet heaven? Earthly beauty? Where hide thee?

Dashwell   Hem, hem.

Loveday   The Cuckold hems. Little thinks he how he is counter-plotted. Hist. Where are you?

Dashwell   Hem, here.

Loveday   Where?

Dashwell   Hist, here, here. Hist.

Loveday   Oh my dear, art thou here? Let me prepare my arms to embrace thee, and give thee the sweet enjoyment of my love! Discover the immodest vigour of my passion. Receive thou the full might and bold expression of my ardour, thus . . .

He whips **Dashwell**.

Dashwell   Ah! Hold. Hold. Hold.

Loveday   I'll take down your courage!

Dashwell   Hold! Help! Help!

Loveday   Make appointments in the dark!

Jane   Wrong my Lady!

She beats him also. Enter **Eugenia** *with a light.*

Doodle   They swinge him unjustly.

Dashwell   Oh, murder. Murder! Murder! Oh!

Doodle   Desist, sir!

Loveday   Do you think it could be my intention ever to wrong so worthy a gentleman as your husband?

Dashwell   Oh hold, hold; you're deceived.

Loveday   No, lewd woman, 'tis you are deceived in your expectation. Now I will go to your husband, and acquaint him with what a chaste good wife you are.

Dashwell   Here, here; bring the candle. I say you are deceived.

Eugenia   Well, husband, have you met with him handsomely?

Loveday   Ha! Madam Eugenia! Who then have I been handling all this while?

Dashwell   Oh wife, I have been lashed and beaten here most unmercifully.

Loveday   Oh Lord, sir; is it you? It was not my intention to thus abuse you, but to punish the lewd behaviour of your wife.

Eugenia   How have you been beaten? Sirrah, I'll have you hanged. First tempt me, then beat my husband!

Loveday   Oh misfortune; have I been injuring you, sir, all this while?

Eugenia   I acquainted my husband with your intentions, and sent him in my place to be revenged of you for your insolence.

Dashwell   Nay, nay, wife; 'twas a mistake. Nay, nay; I am convinced it was well meant.

Wiseacres   Well, well, Mr Dashwell, you have certainly paid him off; ha, ha, ha.

Dashwell   Well, well; talk no more of it.

Doodle   'Tis very suspicious.

Dashwell   He meant no hurt; he did it but to try my wife, for my sake.

Wiseacres   And I fear he has indeed tried her for you, neighbour.

Dashwell   Well, well . . . censure as you please. This misfortune is a great satisfaction to me. I heard your stories from within, and would not yet change my wife for her that a man leapt from her window, nor the Lady No of whom that Gentleman dreamed such a fine dream there, nor one who would have him clamouring at her cellar-hole, ha ha.

Doodle   Nor one who would hide him in her cupboard and cry Devil, forsooth.

Dashwell   What say you?

Doodle   Do you not recognise this apparition?

Dashwell   Who's this? The Devil indeed.

Doodle   Indeed the Devil. Ha!

Dashwell   I'll warrant you a thief, sir, of property or persons, and if the law will not trounce you there are husbands surely shall.

Doodle   Aye, and a ratcatcher should have no complaint when a rat is caught.

Wiseacres   Nor killed neither.

Loveday   Gentlemen, desist. Do not treat him so unkindly as already bears such wounds.

Ramble   I thank you, sir. 'Tis often neighbours want compassion, that the traveller more easily affords. But wait; who's this? Valentine? Valentine Loveday, my friend. How long have you been come from Hamburg?

All (*variously*)   How? Valentine Loveday? And from Hamburg?

Loveday   I am discovered.

Dashwell   My wife's former suitor. Nay then, I fear there's something more in this business than I yet apprehend.

Townley   I fear you have made mischief, Ned.

Dashwell   Pray, sir, how came you to use this trick to get into my service?

Loveday   Sir; the truth is honourable, yet harsh. Some friends of mine, having come to Hamburg, did report to me that Eugenia, since she had married you, had lost her virtuous inclinations. They supposed her disgusted with her marriage.

Dashwell   Ha!

Eugenia   I am neither beholden to them for their opinion, nor you for your belief.

Loveday   Madam, the truth of this slander I resolved to know, purposing never to marry, nor put trust in womankind if she was false. But now I am assured of her virtue and shall not return to Hamburg, but will remain in this City to look myself a wife.

Arabella   He has a quick invention.

Loveday   And now, sir, I hope you are satisfied, and give me your pardon.

Dashwell   Ay, ay. I must be satisfied. Have no thought you could design upon my wife, for it must be remembered you have the assets of but a single man. And she is married, sir, to an Alderman of the City and is thus secured. She has, sir, of her own, not one pound. And must needs be satisfied.

Doodle   Ay, ay Mr Dashwell. You may well scratch your head. For all your wife's virtue you'll see the fruits of her zeal upon your forehead ere long.

Dashwell   I would not yet change my wife's virtue for your wife's wit, Mr Alderman!

Doodle   But neighbour, I think, *consideratis considerandis*, the witty wife is the best of the three.

Dashwell   To that I answer in your own wife's dialect; No.

Wiseacres   Let all be settled then, and let's retire.

Peggy   But Nuncle-Husband . . . In London, dreams are dreams, I know. And gentlemen are not, you say, and so shall I. But Nuncle-Husband rats, I know, will not go up no trees.

Ramble   Here's trouble at its prettiest.

Peggy   So this gentleman is no rat-catcher, and if he be no gentleman neither, I can scarce believe he is a dream, 'cos there he stands and there he is.

Wiseacres   Child, listen now and listen well. I spoke to a conjuror before I went, to conjure up something before your eyes on purpose to make you think as you thought, and to conjure you asleep, and make you dream as you dreamt, and the face of this gentleman, who you had seen at his business in the street entered the dream as you fell sleeping, and the face of this gentleman entered the dream as you were roused. I tell you it was all but a dream, and the conjuror's doing.

Peggy   Then Uncle-Husband, speak to him to conjure up such a thing every night. And let me dream whenever I'm asleep.

Wiseacres   How she torments me.

Peggy   Indeed Uncle-Husband it seemed to me just for all the world as if I had been awake.

Wiseacres   Go. Get you into bed.

Peggy   Yes. But might the conjuror conjure so again?

Wiseacres   No. No, he has taught me now. I'll come and conjure myself.

Peggy   But can you conjure as well as he did?

Wiseacres *strikes* **Peggy**.

Wiseacres   Get you in! Take her away or I'll break your bones.

Aunt   Ah woe. We shall all be hanged. All hanged.

Exeunt **Peggy** *and* **Aunt**.

Dashwell   Now, Mr Alderman I hope you are convinced. This is what comes of a silly wife.

Wiseacres   Pray concern yourself with your zealous wife over there, who has been above at her devotions.

Doodle   Oh ha, ha, ha.

Wiseacres   And you, Brother Alderman, concern yourself with your witty wife who has done No disloyal thing and therefore has made you No cuckold!

Dashwell   I will not be moved to change my opinion. I have business in the morning. Wife. Good night, Gentlemen.

Doodle   Nor shall I be otherwise converted. Come wife. Good night.

Wiseacres   I shall never more trust a wife's simplicity, but from henceforth I'll keep her under lock and key.

Exeunt **Dashwell**, **Doodle** *and* **Wiseacres**.

Arabella   Sirs, I find you are the charitable men who have instructed the innocent.

Ramble   Madam; he is the man.

Arabella   And so he is. And Eugenia, I now spy the hypocrite under the veil of devotion. I always had too good an opinion of your wit to believe you were in earnest. Let us meet tomorrow, each confess the whole truth, and laugh heartily at the folly of our husbands.

Eugenia   With mine you see how smoothly matters went. He is a cuckold. Cudgelled yet content.

Arabella   And what will you with the fine Loveday?

Eugenia   He has my heart, and shall keep it always.

Dashwell (*within*)   Wife!

Loveday   Come, fair Eugenia. Let us take this chance and fly.

Eugenia   To where, my love?

Loveday   Where'er the sun shall rise each day, or every evening set its gleam upon our union.

Eugenia   Loveday, though I do cherish thee, my life is of this City, and this good house. Whilst your figure is fine, it is but paltry clothed. Love may embrace but ne'er sustain our lives. You must live thus; alone, yet in my heart.

Exit **Eugenia**.

Ramble   Now I find I have lost all my mistresses. Eugenia repulses me e'en more curtly than she did thee, Loveday. And you, Frank, have leapt into that lady's saddle before me. But I am sure of my pretty fool when e'er I can come at her.

Townley   'Til then, Ned, to the bottle?

Ramble   Ay; lead on. Madam . . .

Arabella   Struggle not for a fine farewell, sir. Take you your cue from the able Eugenia.

Ramble   Madam, as you would have it.

Exeunt **Ramble** *and* **Townley**.

Arabella   Think you, sir, that love is a greater thing than barter? Think you we women prize our hearts more cheaply than our determined lives?

Loveday   I do love the fair Eugenia.

Arabella   If you would play the game further, sir, it must be a solo hand.

Loveday   Your servant, madam, and ever hers.

Exit **Loveday**.

Epilogue

Spoken by Arabella.

And so, rouse up, ye drowsie cuckolds of our isle.
We see your aching hearts behind your forced smiles.
Haste hence like bees, back to your little hives
And drive away the hornets from your wives.
And like the noble deer does carry antlers high,
Be proud of the chase you would deny.
For what all men in their hidden tender hearts discern
Is the route they would travel, their wives have also learned.
And for each bold encounter in which men loudly glory
In some more secret place a gentler tryst plays out the
woman's story.
And what provoked the poet to this fury?
Perhaps his wit springs not from wisdom but from injury.
All lovers fall to earth that first seemed Heaven sent.
Passion, faith, devotion; all are quickly spent.
All's one; our sins upon us, we'll never be content.

End.

Printed in the USA
CPSIA information can be obtained
at www.ICGtesting.com
LVHW041058171024
794057LV00001B/138

9 780413 729507